Coping:
Attention Deficit Disorder

Mary Ellen Beugin

Detselig Enterprises Ltd.
Calgary, Alberta

Canadian Cataloguing in Publication Data

Beugin, Mary Ellen.
Coping

    Includes biographical references.
    ISBN 1-55059-013-8

    1. Attention deficit disorders. 2. Hyperactive children. I. Title.
RJ496. A86B48 1990   618.92'8589   C90-091429-7

Detselig Enterprises Limited
P.O. Box G 399
Calgary, Alberta, T3A 2G3

Printed in Canada

SAN 115-0324   ISBN 1-55059-013-8

Dedication

To my husband, Brian, and my children, Jeff and Lisa, for their patience and support during the many trials and tribulations in the course of writing this book.

Acknowledgements

I would like to thank David Elliot, M.D., and Harvey Brink, chartered psychologist, for reading sections of this book, offering comment, and encouraging me in writing this book from the point of view of a parent and teacher. I would also like to thank the following school administrators, teachers and parents who read parts of the book and offered valuable comment and encouragement: Albert Lougheed, Jean Mudd, Judi May, Diana Dixon and Shari Mathison.

Disclaimer

This book is not intended as a substitute for seeking medical or psychological treatment of attention deficit disorder (hyperactivity). If such problems are suspected, it is urged that a medical doctor be consulted and, possibly, a mental health professional as well. Neither the author nor publisher accept any legal or moral responsibility, nor any liability, for actions taken by parents or others that are not based on the advice of a physician.

The area of attention deficit disorder is one of considerable controversy. The information and views expressed in this book are those found to be most prominent and current in the literature reviewed by the author, and those consistent with the experiences of the author.

Names and identifying characteristics of children profiled in this book have been changed. Because children presently identified as ADD are predominantly boys the male pronoun will be used when referring to an ADD child.

Table of Contents

Introduction

Jay's problems intensified when he started school. As a baby, he'd been more demanding than his two older brothers, but his experienced parents took this in their stride. Nor were they unduly disturbed by his high activity level and constant mischieviousness as a toddler. As he grew older, his unruly and disobedient behavior, as well as his bossiness toward playmates, caused some concern, but he was an enthusiastic, fun-loving child and his forcefulness was attributed to the fact he was "all boy" and "had a mind of his own." His parents noticed, too, that neither punishment nor encouragement had much affect on his behavior, but they hoped he would settle down once he went to school.

However, in grade one he was expected to sit in a desk without bothering others, listen to the teacher for an extended time, and complete work with reasonable care. This was asking of him exactly what he couldn't do: sit still, attend at will, and work in a careful, organized manner. Instead, he squirmed and bounced in his desk and fell off his chair in the reading circle. When the time came to pay attention to the teacher, he played with objects in his desk, poked or otherwise disturbed the children around him, or was seen to be off in a world of his own. Given seatwork to complete, he needed prompting to start and to keep on working, and then often rushed through it and turned in work with omissions and careless errors. It was apparent to the teacher that he was a bright child, but he did not live up to expectations. She found him likable, but lamented it was a shame such a bright boy wouldn't pay attention or sit still and do his work.

Though Jay was enthusiastic and friendly on the playground, he wanted things to go his way, and he let his frustration be known if he didn't win whatever game was being played. Before

1

long, the other children began to shun him because of his loud, bossy manner and his poor sportsmanship.

Off to a poor start in grade one due to inattentiveness and disorganization, Jay fell further and further behind as he proceeded through school. Though teachers generally found him engaging and likable, he had difficulty following rules and had to be reprimanded more often than other students. Relationships with his playmates continued to be stormy, and sometimes he had no one to play with. At home, his parents struggled in trying to discipline him and had realized by now that his difficulties were long term. Added to the frequent conflict here were battles over homework as his mother tried to help him in his areas of weakness.

Because of his obvious brightness and his good fund of information, he continued to be passed from grade to grade though his reading and writing skills were well below standard. It was felt holding him back would not solve his problems or improve his attitude which was becoming increasingly negative toward school.

By grade nine Jay was still reading at a grade six level. Never one to quietly nurse his frustrations, and into the turbulence of adolescent rebellion, he had by now gained the reputation of being a "bad actor." His continuing inattentiveness and poor work habits were seen to be the result of low motivation, so counselling was tried in an effort to improve his attitude and behavior.

When this didn't work, the school tried dealing with his academic problems by holding him in grade nine for a second year. By now most of his excess activity had calmed, but he remained inattentive, disorganized and easily frustrated, and he couldn't read much of the required material. Not knowing how to deal with his disruptive, rude behavior, the school system shunted him from school to school, offering alternate programs and teachers. Jay, however, solved the problem for them when on his sixteenth birthday, the legal age for such decisions, he quit school.

Alienated from the mainstream of his peers and in constant conflict with his family, he became involved in delinquent activities which attracted the attention of the police. He was accused and warned about various minor misdemeanors, but managed to stay out of detention. In some ways, his life had become easier as he was no longer faced with daily failure, but years of conflict and failure had lowered his self-esteem. As well, his poor organization, low frustration tolerance, and need to run things his way, along with generally poor social skills, continued to mark his life.

Through family connections he was able to get a job, but it didn't last long. He went on to a variety of other jobs. Though bright, young, and in many ways able, he has been unable to hold steady employment. His personal life shows a similar picture. Although he maintained a brief relationship with a girl which resulted in a daughter, both the girl and his daughter are now out of his life. He has been unable to form other stable, adult relationships.

Jay's story is not an unusual one for children affected with what was called hyperactivity, and now has been renamed *attention deficit disorder with hyperactivity.* However, in the past ten years, there has been new research in this area and experts now suggest the possibility of a happier, more productive life for children such as Jay.

Some of Jay's problems in school may have been caused by perceptual or language problems often called learning disabilities, but this possibility was not investigated, and the area of learning disabilities is not directly addressed in this book. However, it should be kept in mind that children with attention deficit disorder may also have specific language or perceptual problems which should be investigated as well. Attention deficit disorder is, however, a primary impediment to learning in itself and affected children, like Jay, are typically chronic underachievers.

This book will view close-up in their homes and at school a number of children with attention deficit disorder (ADD). It will deal with the nature of ADD and the interrelated learning and behavior problems that emerge from it. It will examine the new research and expert opinion that offers hope for these children. The importance of treatment for such children, for whom otherwise, the outlook may be poor, will be addressed.

The ADD child is not the only victim of his disorder. Often the presence of such a child can have severe effects on the parents and family and, to a lesser extent, on his teachers and classmates. Parents and teachers spend their days interacting with these children and are on the front lines in providing much of the help these children might receive. In the back of their minds they may hold grave concerns about the future for such a child. This book will look at the problems of living and dealing with an ADD child on a daily basis and at the long-term perspective for these children. It will examine the feelings and views of all involved and encourage open communication and support between home and school.

Having a child creates a vulnerability, the depth of which did not exist before. Few things can tear into the heart like watching one's child in pain. We all want our children to be the best they can be — to fulfill their dreams and ours. Few things can equal the anguish of watching the hopes for a decent life for our child die a slow death. This pain can only be added to by the knowledge that everyone blames us for this tragedy, and by the deep-down niggling sense that maybe, just maybe, for some reason we do not understand, they are right. Such is the plight of the ADD child and his parents. This book sheds new light and hope on this sad family situation.

It will draw on information from the most recent literature on ADD. More importantly, it will share insights gained in my experience with my own child who has been diagnosed as having ADD, and from teaching many children with attentional and behavior problems. As well, it will share understandings I have gained from other parents and teachers in their struggle to come to terms with and help these difficult children.

1

Children with
Attention Deficit Disorder:

Who are They?

Like other children, children with ADD are individuals, each with his own particular style and personality. Typically, they have many positive qualities: they are fun-loving, outgoing and friendly, and have a keen sense of humor. Usually they are energetic and show an enquiring attitude, great enthusiasm and leadership qualities. Many are bright.

Tragically, their strong, positive qualities are often overshadowed by some disabilities. These children are unable to control their behavior within acceptable limits and focus their energy in a positive, purposeful way. This leads them to problems with adults, with their peers, and with their learning, in short: with every aspect of their lives.

These are children for whom parents and teachers often see considerable possibilities — "If only they would control themselves." Yet, too often, their talents are wasted as they run into problems with authority figures, become social outcasts, and fail academically. The inconsistency of their behavior and the attitudes they develop often lead one to believe they could do better if they tried or were properly disciplined. And indeed, to some extent, discipline and experiences can affect their ADD behavior, but poor discipline and life experiences are never the cause of it (Wender 1987, 27).

Children with ADD are believed to constitute 3 to 10 percent of school-age children (Wender 1987, 3). There are likely one or two of them in every school classroom, although they are not

5

commonly diagnosed as having ADD, but more likely, as having emotional or behavioral problems rooted in the home (Wender 1987, 18). Boys are believed to outnumber girls on a six to one to a nine to one ratio. It is not known why. Experts believe the answer will ultimately lie in the same reason boys are more likely than girls to have learning disorders, mental retardation, psychosis and other psychological disorders (Barkley 1985, 162).

The preschool child sitting in his mother's shopping cart who, having touched everything he can reach, for no reason anyone can fathom, begins to kick the unsuspecting customer beside him; the elementary school child in the restaurant kicking the table as he squirms in his chair, who complains loudly because his food hasn't arrived immediately; the teenager on the bus, poking, shoving, and clowning, who fails to pick up cues from his age-mates that they don't appreciate his performance — all of these may be children with ADD.

Children with ADD sometimes behave in ways that show a lack of care and discretion: they do things that other children, being more cautious, never consider doing — things like kicking a stranger or hanging precariously over a rail two floors above a cement sidewalk. At other times, ADD children carry troublesome behavior to an extreme. They whine, fight, and get into things more frequently and with a greater intensity than do other children. They are like cars with their motors always running and no awareness of speed limit or other traffic regulations. On top of this, neither rewards nor punishments seem helpful in changing unwanted behavior in these difficult children.

Two Types of Attention Deficit

Experts have recently delineated two types of attention deficit disorders: those with hyperactivity, and those without hyperactivity. The key element in ADD is seen to be a weakness in attending and focusing skills. Thus, ADD children without hyperactivity may have severe problems with attention and concentration (and associated organizational skills), but don't exhibit excessive movement. Nor are they usually aggressive or disruptive. Their academic, social and emotional problems may, however, be just as debilitating as those of the more active ADD child. These quieter children, many of them girls, are less often identified and, consequently, it's not known what their numbers might be.

While all ADD children have problems to varying degrees with attention and concentration, other characteristics may be absent or vary in intensity from child to child. Some children are more active, some are more aggressive, some are strongly both, some are neither.

Because this book focuses on the behaviors that cause trouble for ADD children and those around them, I will use as examples children who show high levels of all troublesome behaviors. I will speak only of ADD or, alternately, of hyperactivity when I am referring to the active, aggressive elements of the disorder. However, keep in mind that excess movement, restlessness and aggressiveness are not always an integral part of ADD.

Excessive Movement

For those who move excessively, it is not the movement in itself that gets them into trouble, but rather, the inappropriate timing for the movement. Seen in a free-play situation such as on a playground, these children do not move any more than many other energetic children. It is when asked to sit still, such as at the dinner table or in school, that their inability to curtail their movement causes problems. This is not to say that they are always moving, as many can sit quite still for at least a little while. However, these children are often seen to be giggling, jiggling and squirming, if not falling out of their chairs or getting up to walk or run around.

They are the children at school whose pencils are always in need of sharpening, and who make excess trips to the water fountain and washroom. Their movement distracts others, as does the noise that often accompanies it. If they aren't whispering to others or talking out of turn, they are imitating cars or making other noises. Other students complain of the constant distractions, and this is one reason why they tend to shun these students. By the time these children reach adolescence, for most the excess movement has disappeared, but a feeling of restlessness may remain as well as other serious problems. Many times, these children are poor sleepers. They have difficulty settling down at night and/or sleeping through the night, and toss and turn while they are asleep.

Impulsivity

Impulsivity, the inability to stop and think before acting, creates substantial problems for these children and those around them. ADD children interrupt others who are speaking, butt into games or into lines, and grab toys or other items they may want. They do this often and beyond the age when other children have learned better manners. Impulsivity, too, makes them accost strangers in a way no thinking child would do, such as happened to the unfortunate customer at the store. Needless to say, this type of behavior does not endear them to others. Their peers fight back or complain about them and eventually begin to avoid them. Teachers are not inclined to look favorably on their frequent calling out of answers which accompanies their other disruptions in the classroom. In addition, their impulsive behavior can be dangerous and frightening to their parents, as these children may, without thinking, dash into the street or climb on high objects where the foothold is precarious.

Short Attention Span

Short attention spans cause these children the most trouble at school, but at home it will be noticed that they seldom finish anything and tend to shift activities often. This can be most frustrating to an adult who attempts to share an activity with them. It is another reason for problems with playmates who like to finish a game or spend extended time playing with toys or completing something such as a puzzle: ADD children rush on to a new activity while other children their age are still involved.

Confoundingly, these children can often focus for considerable time on something new or in which they are keenly interested. In fact, there may be times when ADD children become so engrossed in an activity that it is almost impossible to draw them away from it. So it would seem the problem is not in the attending so much as in attending "at will." These children seem to have an exceedingly low boredom threshold, and once disinterest sets in, they can't seem to "make" themselves pay attention like the rest of us can. They can't seem to force concentration. This is true even when they know it is important to attend or when there are penalties for non-attention.

Carrying on any type of conversation with these children can be a challenge. They often seem to have trouble following a channel of thought as their minds flit to totally unrelated subjects. One often has the sense that they are not with you, even though they may be looking directly at you.

The problems in the less structured settings of home and play are magnified many times when ADD children attend school. As mentioned in the example of Jay, school demands just the abilities these children don't have. This is particularly evident in the area of attending. If not toe-tapping or distracting others, these children appear to be daydreaming and, if called upon, often have no idea what the teacher was talking about. They are regularly distracted by anything and everything that goes on around them and often by their own thoughts. They can't maintain focus and concentration and need to be brought back to task often.

When given work to do they rush through it, and in many instances, the teacher has to stay on their case to get them to finish it. When finished, it is usually messy, sloppily done, and contains omissions and careless errors, this inferior product being the result of the speed at which it was done, as well as the lack of sustained attention to it.

Lack of Social Skills

As well as turning off other children with their excess movement and impulsive behaviors, ADD children are loud and bossy and seem to have a strong need to dominate others and win whatever game is being played. They want to always choose the activity or game (and to change to a new one as they see fit).

They will often attempt to change the rules of a game in order to win. If that doesn't work, they may claim points they obviously didn't gain, or accuse others of cheating. They seem to have such an overwhelming need to win that they see the facts in a very egocentric way. They may honestly believe that the facts are as they call them: that those who disagree are dishonest and out to get them.

Many are also inveterate teasers who frequently "bug" and harass others, then seem oblivious to the feelings and reactions of their victims. Although they generally crave friendship, they are their own worst enemies when it comes to maintaining it. They are often outgoing and have little difficulty initiating friendship, but their behavior soon alienates others. Having little ability to empathize, they don't seem to pick up on hints or even direct statements from peers about their behavior. They may want friendship desperately and cry desolately when friends they have offended leave. Yet, the next day in the same situation, they will repeat their offensive behavior, the friends will leave again, and again they will be heartbroken. This may happen repeatedly until no friends come around.

Most of these children are not, in the beginning at least, mean or vindictive (Wender 1987, 21). They do get into more than their share of arguments and fights because of their domineering behavior, but they do not set out to harm or annoy anyone. Adults often see these children as generally friendly and likable. However, these children also face a great deal of disapproval from adults and peers alike, and their self-esteem lowers as they grow older. Whether or not they become mean and vindictive may depend on the degree of disapproval and the way their misbehavior is handled.

Rob's mother remembers well her first turn as mother helper at three-year-old Rob's playschool. On that occasion, after much boisterous, overbearing interaction on Rob's part, it came time for students to sit on a wooden bench beside the table for their juice and snack. Just as everyone was comfortably settled in, Rob stood on the bench and poured a glass of apple juice on the head of the girl sitting beside him. He did it in a fun-loving way, as he saw the little girl as a good friend of his. Indeed, she was a tolerant little soul who often played with him. In discussing the matter with his mother, the playschool teacher listed a number of instances of Rob's inappropriate behavior. However, she finished with saying, "But he has such a good little heart!" Rob's mother has kept these words in the front of her mind in many a dark hour.

Negative, Disobedient Behavior

Although not mean and vindictive, a good number of these children resist authority and have difficulty following rules. Having a strong need to dominate and boss other children, they vigorously object to being bossed themselves by anyone, including adults. They actively oppose and argue with parents and/or teachers when requested to do a task. When required to do activities not of their choice, they whine and complain. A frequent area of conflict with parents is over chores and cleaning up after themselves. Conflict is more intense and frequent than with an average child in these matters. At school, they complain that work is boring, or they may want to do it their own way, sometimes to lessen the work, and sometimes for no discernable reason.

Some seem to have the attitude that no one can tell them what to do and will consistently push limits. They might argue and complain for fifteen minutes that they don't have time to clear the dishes from the table because a TV show they want to watch is starting. This, when it would have taken three minutes to clear the table. Repeatedly, they will argue and complain until sent to their rooms, though this means they will miss an activity completely. Although they may dearly want money, they will go without their allowance for a year rather than do chores without complaint.

They often resist their punishment as well, having to be dragged kicking and screaming to their rooms and locked in to keep them there. If physical punishment is used, they may hit and kick parents back and some seem to have a relative insensitivity to pain. Then, to the consternation of parents and teachers, they will engage in the same behavior again and again regardless of past consequences.

If one attempts to use normal discipline with these children, consequences and punishments become meaningless because they add up to ridiculous, unenforceable amounts due to the number of misbehaviors. No wonder oppositional, disobedient and sassy behavior is the most commonly reported problem by both parents and teachers of these children, and is the most common reason for the referral of these children to mental health clinics (Barkley 1985, 161).

Low Frustration Tolerance

The low level of frustration tolerance of children with ADD gives them the reputation of being hot-tempered and cry babies. When younger, they have an immediate tantrum the minute they don't get what they want, whether it be food, a toy, or permission to do an activity. Later, their domineering and oppositional behavior is teamed with a torrent of screaming and crying if they don't immediately get their way.

Darrel was an extremely fast eater from day one. His mother remembers when she began to spoon feed him Pablum. He would gulp a spoonful of the porridge, then before she could refill the spoon and get it again to his mouth, he would begin to scream. Try as she might, she couldn't feed him fast enough to prevent the intermittent, frustrated screams, until one day she discovered that using two spoons and filling one as she put the other in his mouth would do the trick.

Besides having a lower tolerance for frustration, these children react to it more violently than other children. Some seem to go completely wild. In the words of four-year-old David's mother, "He just screams and goes berserk. I may as well save my breath. It's as if there's no one home." This exploding fury frequently occurs when a child is disciplined or otherwise thwarted. And indeed, it seems there is "no one home" as efforts are made to subdue or calm the child and he seems to have blotted out everything but his rage. This may relate to the reason that these children seem not to learn from punishment. They are too involved in their own volatile emotions to appreciate the reason for the punishment and learn from it.

David's mother recounted many instances when David's anger became so intense that any attempt to deal with him resulted in his escalating, blind fury. Perhaps the most vivid illustration of the excess nature and tenacity of his responses is in the following story recounted by his mother of when he was upset by being stung by wasps.

When camping in the woods with the family, David was given permission to go to a nearby tree house with an eight-year-old friend. His mother said she always knew where David was, even in the woods, by his constant yelling and noise. Sure enough, she could soon hear yelling coming from the direction of the tree house. Hearing nothing unusual, she went on with her activities.

About ten minutes later, the distraught eight-year-old arrived to say that young David had fallen from the treehouse and had landed on a nest of yellow-jacket wasps. The friend had run some distance from the nest. He said he kept calling and calling to David to run and get away. But David had sat there screaming, making no effort to retreat from the wasps.

He had more than fifty stings on his face, head and upper body; his mother pulled stingers out of his eyelids and from inside his ears. The next day, both eyes were swollen shut and more stingers were found in his hair. Yet, he showed no fear of wasps after that day; he seemed not to have connected the pain with the wasps. His mother said that frantic screaming was typical of his behavior when he was frustrated, and that punishment had no carry over.

Although they cry, argue and whine at school, and are often seen as immature for their age, these children seem to have somewhat more control here than in the more familiar home situation (as do most children). It is not uncommon, however, for ADD students, in their angry frustration, to throw books and crayons onto the floor and, on occasion, to throw over their desks or throw materials across the room, sometimes accompanied with tantrum-like yelling and screaming.

Excessive, out of control behavior may lead to the vicious cycle of escalating coercive behavior that often develops in family interactions with these children. This will be discussed in Chapter Seven.

Underachievement and Learning Problems

If a child attending a class paid attention to the teacher for thirty seconds or so, then left the room for two or three minutes, then returned for another thirty seconds and continued this pattern for the remainder of the lesson, we would not be surprised if he fell behind the group. When given papers or other seatwork to do, if he applied himself to this task in the same sporadic fashion, and if he was unable to organize his approach to the work, and gave up in frustration when he encountered difficulty, we can understand why he would have further problems.

Such is the case for the ADD child. To all intents and purposes, he is not there much of the time during lessons and when doing seatwork, he works haphazardly, becomes frustrated and gives up easily. It is no wonder that by adolescence most ADD children are chronic underachievers despite normal or superior intelligence. By that time, half of them will have failed one grade and a third will have failed two (Ingersoll 1988, 16).

The inability to focus and maintain concentration is a primary disability of the ADD child and causes much of his learning problems. However, many ADD children also have perceptual and/or language problems usually called learning disabilities and now sometimes called specific developmental delays. According to Larry B. Silver, M.D., former director of the American National Institute of Dyslexia, 85 percent of students who are hyperactive or distractible have perceptual or language problems as well (Silver 1988, 30). Others estimate this correlation to be somewhat lower.

Just as there are some children with ADD who do not have these types of learning disabilities, there are some children with perceptual or language problems who do not have ADD. If a child has both ADD and perceptual/language difficulties (which is often the case), then both of these problems must be addressed. Interventions for learning disabilities are different than those for ADD and are beyond the scope of this book. However, Larry B. Silver's book, *The Misunderstood Child: A Guide For Parents of Learning Disabled Children* (1988), is a good reference in this area.

Whether or not it is called a learning disability, the ADD child, because of his problems with attention and concentration, often has particular difficulty when listening is the main source of information for students. In other words, a lecture approach to teaching and orally given directions will be especially hard for the ADD student. In Chapter Eight we will examine some methods and strategies that allow students to take in information in ways other than listening and thus increase the likelihood of academic success for ADD students.

Variability in Behavior and Performance

Another characteristic, perhaps the most perplexing one for parents and teachers of ADD children, is variability in their behaviors from day to day and week to week. These children tend to be moody and on some days nothing can please them, while on other days everything is relatively sunny and they can be quite agreeable. They may go through relatively stable periods, where you feel at last they've settled down (or perhaps that you've finally hit on the right answer), only to erupt again for no apparent reason.

They tend, also, to perform differently in different situations. Often, in a situation that is new to them, or with people they don't know well, they can be calm and focused. They often perform better on a one to one basis, especially if this isn't used regularly. There is evidence that for all of us, levels of chemicals in the brain change in new situations causing us to become more alert. For these children, this change in brain chemical levels may allow them to attend relatively well.

This variable performance is most frustrating for a teacher who knows a child can do a better job of his work, but doesn't often seem motivated to do so. In these situations, the student's problem seems like an "application" deficit, rather than an "ability" deficit. The refrain, "If only Billy would apply himself!" is oft repeated of these children. Poor performance usually results in criticism of the child both at home and at school and is another source of his lowered self-esteem (Wender 1987, 18).

Coordination Difficulties

About half of all ADD children have some difficulties in coordination (Wender 1987, 19). This may be in fine motor coordination which can mean poor printing and writing as well as difficulties with coloring, cutting, tying shoe laces and like tasks. Some may have mild problems with balance which makes learning to ride a bicycle or skateboard difficult. Others may have poor hand-eye coordination which causes them problems in throwing and catching a ball and in batting activities. However, some ADD children, having no coordination, are very good at sports, while others are good at some sports and activities, but not at others.

Regular Misbehavior versus ADD Misbehavior

As has been stated, ADD children are over-active, impulsive, inattentive, and often disobedient, and have, as well, a low tolerance for frustration and a high need to dominate. These characteristics cause them to behave in ways we don't like — in other words, to misbehave. Yet all children misbehave and all children show many of these traits some of the time. This being so, how do we distinguish between "regular misbehavior" and that which goes beyond into the "hyperactive misbehavior" range?

behavior appropriate to age

It has been noticed that the behavior of the ADD child often resembles behavior of a much younger child. Whereas most two-year-olds when frustrated will lie on the floor and have a down-and-out tantrum with yelling, kicking and screaming, by the time they are four or five most have given up these tactics. Assuming that this behavior has not been reinforced by giving the child what he wants or extra attention when he has a tantrum, the ADD child still continues to have extreme tantrums long after peers have given them up.

While we wouldn't expect a two-year-old to sit still for long to watch TV, a movie at a theater, or a circus, we might expect a four or five year old to be able to do this. The hyperactive four- or five-year-old has difficulty even at the circus, where — after looking at each new act for about ten seconds — he tends to create his own mini circus by standing up and running around; poking or pushing those around him; attempting to climb under the seats; bothering strangers; rocking, kicking and jumping complete with sound effects; begging for treats; needing to go to the bathroom several times; and talking incessantly. Here it seems that the noise and excitement, rather than grabbing his attention as it does that of other children, sets him off into energetic, purposeless activity. He will likely have a tantrum or two as well when denied treats or stopped from doing something. Some regular five-year-olds may show some of these behaviors if they are playing with friends and have not been admonished to sit quietly without bothering others, but their activity has purpose in terms of the give and take of play activity and is appropriate to the extent it has been allowed.

Many regular preschoolers are pretty active and can spend a good part of the day running about, yelling noisily, and exploring. Yet by five or six, most have settled enough to sit quietly in a desk for half an hour at a time if they are told to do so. The school-age hyperactive child has trouble with this, and, though he may not get up and run around, he is often moving and making noise in ways that distract and interrupt others. The delay in self-control follows as the child gets older. The ADD child in grade four may have the ability to organize himself and concentrate comparable to a regular grade one student. Thus, these students fail to live up to age-appropriate expectations.

intensity and frequency of misbehavior

Not only do hyperactive children resemble children of a younger age, they also engage in many undesirable behaviors with a greater intensity or degree of severity than other children, and misbehave more frequently than others.

Looking again at tantrums can illustrate these differences. The regular two-year-old will perhaps have three or four good tantrums a day, whereas, the hyperactive two-year-old sometimes has twenty or thirty. If you follow expert advice to ignore tantrums as a way of demonstrating to the child that tantrums will not get him what he wants, the regular child will usually quieten down after some time.

If you attempt to ignore the hyperactive child, he will scoot himself over to you or, if this isn't possible, get up off the floor (never missing a beat in his screaming) and proceed to hit and kick you, forcing you to take some action. If you leave the room, he will follow you. If you go into another room and lock the door, he will pound on the door, often damaging it.

When you take him kicking and screaming to his room (and lock him there, as otherwise he will be right back out), he will kick holes in the wall and bash holes in the door with his toys. When you spank him, he will fight you and continue his screaming. You will soon realize that you can't humanely spank a child twenty or thirty times a day. If you spank him long enough and hard enough to stop him for any amount of time, you will probably be well into the realm of child abuse.

intense, frequent and "out of bounds" behavior

Oftentimes, the misbehavior of the hyperactive child is not only more intense and frequent than that of others, but goes beyond behavior other children display because they are more cautious (or they may remember what happened the last time they tried something of the sort). To get an idea of the extremity of this behavior, let's follow a preschool ADD child through a variety of experiences you might have with him.

You take this child to the store and he grabs items off the shelves, runs up and down the aisles, and whines and screams loudly and conspicuously for things he wants. You take him to a children's movie and after being shushed and admonished many times, he suddenly tackles the man seated in front of him, giving him a surprise bear hug from behind. You take him to the library, and he begins to push the books off the shelves as you and the librarian attempt to catch him.

You take him to the swimming pool and he's up in the lifeguard chair before you have time to follow him out of the water. You take him to the playground; he runs up and over the equipment (and any people who happen to be in his way), stops at the sandbox and proceeds to throw sand at some children playing peacefully on the other side.

You take him to the doctor's office and after throwing all the books from the waiting room table onto the floor, he attempts to open all the drawers, turn on the water, and pull equipment off the walls. You take him to the hospital for a test which requires the insertion of a needle into his arm, and the staff are clearly not happy when they find a doctor, an orderly and a nurse cannot, between the three of them, hold him still enough to put the needle into his arm.

You take him to a restaurant and, just when you think you have him busy eating, he sees the waitress bending over the next table. In the wink of an eye, he has reached over, put his fork under her dress and is yelling, "Yah, yah, yah," as he waves the instrument around inside her skirt. You take him to the company picnic and while you have dared to take a moment to speak to the woman beside you, he has jumped onto the table and is running down its length, much to the consternation of other picnickers. You leave him playing in the yard that borders on the driveway, and your neighbor calls to say she has seen him filling up the gas tank of the family stationwagon with water from the hose.

Of course, during all these little adventures you are watching him like a hawk, but if you have a baby in your arms or are attempting to get something done, you will have a very difficult time controlling him.

The constraints and structure of school tone down the behavior of all children somewhat. However, ADD children go beyond the boundaries of regular school behavior as well — often to the same degree they overstep boundaries in other situations. Of course, less active, less impulsive ADD children will not display all of this behavior, but their inattention, their emotionality, and their social ineptness will deviate from that of other children to a noticeable degree.

Conclusion

In conclusion to this chapter, we will look at a final example of the increased intensity and frequency of problem behaviors in ADD children and the effect this has on those who care for them. We will look at their sleep patterns, since the sleep patterns of hyperactive youngsters often mirror their other difficulties. Just as constant monitoring, disciplining, and frustration over the inability to moderate behavior in these children is stressful and wearing to their parents, so is dealing with their sleeplessness.

Once past six or seven months, most babies sleep through the night fairly regularly. While a parent might be up for several nights in a row with an older teething baby or up two or three times a month with an older baby for various other reasons, most who are not hyperactive sleep through the night fairly regularly by the time they are a year old.

With the hyperactive older baby, a parent is often up two or three times every night until the baby is well over a year old. Then for the next few years the parent may be up at least once every night with the child. This is on top of the difficulty one often has getting the child to sleep, which may not be until midnight or one in the morning, and the early rising of such a child, which is often at six or seven in the morning. (And it is in addition to being up, on occasion, with other children in the family.)

As well, the hyperactive child is regularly difficult to comfort. One may give him a bottle which he will drink before he resumes screaming. One may walk the floor with a fighting, screaming baby. One may try to rock him. One may give him medications suggested by the doctor. All will be to little avail. At last, one may just listen to him scream. And he will scream almost every night for years.

Imagine, if you can, what it is like to never be permitted to sleep through the night for years. Many parents of hyperactive children will have little difficulty imagining this. Compare this to getting up each night for a few months or so with a regular baby, who is usually able to be comforted, and then, occasionally, throughout the next years. This may help you grasp the difference in intensity and frequency of behavior in the hyperactive child.

Now try to envision the daily havoc and frustration of living with a hyperactive child, then add to this the bone-tiredness born of never getting a good night's sleep. Keeping this picture in mind may help you understand the impotence and the feeble effort sometimes seen in parents trying to cope with an obviously "out of bounds" child. More about the difficulties parents experience will be discussed in Chapter Five.

2

Ages and Stages:

How do ADD Children Change?

Hyperactivity and other ADD behaviors are easiest seen in the preschool and early elementary school child. Even here, they are often mistaken for learned habits resulting from faulty parenting or as reactions to bad experiences. As the child gets older, it becomes harder to see that his problems are the result of a primary weakness in control and focusing skills. This is because for these children, as for all of us, it is less distressing to say, "I don't want to" rather than, "I can't." As well, by this time the child will have experienced considerable failure and conflict, and as he enters puberty his emotional problems will be most noticeable and of greatest concern. Nevertheless, if we try, we can keep in sight the primary deficits in control and focus as we look at how the behaviors and problems of an ADD individual evolve and change throughout his lifespan.

Infancy

Most babies throw their parents for something of a loop with the added demands and responsiblity they bring. ADD children often send their parents on what seems to be an endless roller coaster ride.

Cory's mother remembers his infancy as a noisy, hectic, sleepless nightmare. Fussy and colicy from the beginning, Cory was up several times each night and slept little during the day. Nothing could comfort him. He literally screamed for hours, so much so that neighbors inquired about the crying. The doctor could offer nothing beyond the usual remedies, none of which worked, and the advice that all babies cry. In fact, Cory didn't sleep through the night until he was over four years old, although as he got older he was up less often. He had eczema and was sick often with diarrhea, colds and croup. He had two bouts of bronchitis before the age of one.

Not a cuddly baby, he squirmed, arched his back and often threw his head back, hitting whoever was holding him. He kicked and screamed ferociously when he was held still to have his diaper changed. When he was old enough to grasp objects, he constantly picked up anything he could get his hands on and threw it.

Once able to get onto hands and knees and pull himself up in his crib, he began to move the crib around the bedroom with his rocking and jumping. His mother often found the crib blocking the door when she attempted to enter. Before Cory was two, the crib mattress was demolished and had to be replaced.

As many as 60 to 70 percent of hyperactive children show signs of their difficult temperament before age two (Ingersoll 1988, 8). As in Cory's case, they are often fussy, irregular and unpredictable in habits. They sleep less than other infants, and are typically up during the night more frequently and over a longer time than other infants. They are difficult to hold or comfort, cry more, and often don't adjust well to change. Allergies are common and there are often early and repeated bouts of sickness, especially colds, upper respitory infections and ear problems (Ingersoll 1988, 9).

The Preschool Years

The two most common phrases heard from parents of pre-school-age ADD children are: "He never walks, he runs," and "I can't turn my back for a minute." Some youngsters, after a relatively calm, uneventful babyhood, become noticeably more active, aggressive and disobedient as they enter early childhood. Initially, this may seem an extreme version of the "terrible twos." However, much to the consternation of their parents, these children don't settle as they become older. Other ADD children continue to show the active, demanding pattern of behavior they exhibited as babies.

After a difficult babyhood, Peter became an overcharged dynamo as he entered toddlerhood. His parents plugged all unused plugs, secured all cupboard doors with childproof locks, moved all ornaments and other things out of reach, blocked off the living room where plants were endangered, and otherwise childproofed the house. In spite of these arrangements, his mother had trouble getting her housework done because of the constant attention Peter required. If he couldn't find something to pound, pull apart or otherwise damage, he was demanding she play or get something for him. Even watching TV couldn't keep him occupied for more than five minutes at a time.

On the go all day, he still woke up once or twice each night. His babyhood fussiness seemed to have transformed into endless tantrums, occasioned by being stopped from an activity or not getting attention or whatever else he wanted. His mother explained that with several tantrums per hour, he often had between twenty and thirty per day. Ignoring him, sending him to his room, or punishment had no affect on this.

It was an embarassment to take him anywhere because he was into everything. When restrained or denied something he flew into a tantrum. He hit, grabbed toys and was otherwise aggressive toward would-be playmates, and soon became an unwelcome guest at the homes of family friends. Nor was it easy to find anyone to babysit him.

Once he was past his "terrible twos," his parents had hoped for some moderation in behavior. His father commented, however, that with Peter, "The terrible twos just seemed to go on forever." And indeed, this is the experience of many parents of these children. The "terrible two" stage seems to extend to the throes of "adolescent rebellion."

The preschool years can be exhausting ones for the care-givers of such a child. These are the years during which ADD children are at the greatest risk of child abuse because they are underfoot all day and can be so difficult to manage (Gold 1986, 11). Because of their high speed, inquisitiveness and lack of caution, hyperactive children are more accident prone and are seen more often at emergency clinics. Toilet training is often difficult, and many are not bowel trained until after three years of age and continue to have accidents long after their peers do not (Ingersoll 1988, 11).

The Elementary School Years

Scott's teacher shook her head. Scott had been in her classroom an hour, during which time he'd spent more time avoiding work than doing it. At the beginning of the lesson he had seemed interested, so much so that she'd reprimanded him several times for not raising his hand to speak. From there, he had spent the rest of the lesson looking out the window, fiddling with something in his desk, whispering to the child ahead of him or tapping his feet.

When it came time to do pencil and paper work, he had to be reminded several times to get started and do his work. Then he rushed through it, missing several questions, and his writing was such that many answers were barely legible.

Now she could see him proceeding down the hall to his next class. He had already picked up a pencil dropped by another child and had thrown it several feet down the hall. The other child had objected, but Scott seemed to think it was all in good fun. Now he draped his hands over the shoulders of a student ahead of him. When the student pushed him away he looked surprised and hurt, and pushed back. After settling the altercation, Scott's teacher commented, "He really means no harm, but he's such a pest!"

At school, as these children come under continual surveillance, their problems become more evident, and they are reprimanded and receive other negative feedback more often. Because of their emotionality and lack of control over their behavior, they are often labelled immature in early school years. Later, teachers may suspect serious emotional problems because of their emotionality and their frequent fascination with weapons, war and gruesome monsters (Ingersoll 1988, 13). As well, they are disorganized, forgetful and messy, and demand more than their fair share of immediate teacher attention.

As they progress through elementary school, problems in learning may become evident (although some make it to adolescence before these are noticed). Though the difficulties are often blamed on attitude and motivation, many will at this time receive some help with their academic weaknesses. Still, their spotty perfomance often causes teachers to feel they could do better if they tried.

Because they tend to be so domineering, they often end up playing with younger children or with older children who may be more tolerant, or they play alone. Often their peers will tease them or pick on them because they delight in provoking those with explosive tempers, and because these children are generally unpopular and have low self-esteem.

As ADD children become alienated from their peers, they may begin bragging, lying, fighting and stealing (Ingersoll 1988, 14). Now their peers may get back at them with more teasing and put-downs and scapegoating. These emotionally volatile children become caught in a vicious cycle of aggression and counter-aggression and usually end up the losers.

Meanwhile, at home there are arguements over homework and chores. There are angry outbursts as frustration with school mounts and parents pressure them to improve their performance. These children blame others for their plight and may complain that teachers are mean and no one likes them, but when parents attempt to discuss this, they show little insight into their part in the problem and will stubbornly insist that peers and teachers are at fault. Although they generally fail to see (or admit, even to themselves) how their behavior leads to their difficulties, many begin to secretly believe that they are stupid, unlovable and worthless.

Adolescence

According to Barbara Ingersoll, Ph.D., in her book, *Your Hyperactive Child* (1988), about 20 percent of ADD children will have outgrown all symptoms of attention deficit disorder by the time they reach puberty. However, many of these will continue to have problems because of previous criticism and their experiences as social outcasts. Academic failure may have scarred them, so even though they now have no learning handicap, they are turned off by school and may quit (Wender 1987, 38). Their self-esteem will be low, and they may have well established antisocial behaviors such as lying and stealing.

For most of the remaining group of hyperactive children, the high level of activity will have decreased. The tapping and squirming may remain and/or there may be a feeling of restlessness. Because they are not as active, these children are now less conspicuous. Some of the associated problems may have diminished as well. However, for many, serious behavioral, emotional, and/or learning problems remain (Wender 1987, 25).

As ADD students enter junior high school, problems typically intensify because more independence, responsibility and organizational skills are required. Academic problems may become serious and get some heed now — if they have not before. At this stage, however, emotional and social problems are apt to get more attention because teachers know peer relationships are crucial at this age, and because acting-out behaviors will probably have worsened.

A pattern of conflict with parents, teachers and peers is usually well established by now. These patterns and the ADD child's low self-esteem are now complicated by the stresses and difficulties of adolescence. The rebellion, arguing, and moodiness of normal adolescence is amplified.

There are likely to be "battles royal" at home. Now the physical size of the child becomes important as he is too big to be taken physically to his room or stopped physically from harmful actions. It may be difficult for parents to find recourse when a child flatly refuses to do something. The child may now physically threaten his parents during fights. He may threaten to run away in times of extreme conflict — and may carry through on his threat.

A significant number of ADD adolescents become involved in antisocial behaviors such as vandalism and stealing (Ingersoll 1988, 17). Many become involved in drug or alcohol use. In addition, ADD adolescents are more often depressed than other teenagers. Some researchers say that this is because of the constant conflict and failure they have experienced, while others say sadness and demoralization are part of the disorder (Ingersoll 1988, 18).

Adulthood

About one-half of ADD adolescents continue to have mild to severe problems as adults. Often these are the same problems as in adolescence; only the settings have changed. They may continue to have problems with attention and concentration, especially when the tasks are not interesting to them. Poor organization, forgetfulness and poor frustration tolerance may now plague them in their work and personal lives. Their hot tempers may cause problems on the job and may lead to serious abuse of their own children (Ingersoll 1988, 20). Often there will be trouble establishing stable family relationships and holding a steady job.

Many will describe their childhoods as unhappy and continue to have low self-esteem. Emotional highs and lows continue for many. Some become depressed or suffer from psychotic disorders (Ingersoll 1988, 21), while others engage in serious antisocial behavior which brings them into conflict with the law. Unfortunately, some continue or begin drug and alcohol abuse at this time.

Conclusion

Looking at the life pattern of children with attention deficit disorder, we can see problems that impact seriously on the quality of life for both them and their families. At school, the problems of these children directly affect the work of teachers and other students who are grouped with them. Besides that, the long term outcome for many of these children is not one that any parent or teacher would wish for a child. Without help, even those who outgrow their ADD are often left with lowered self-esteem and associated problems.

Finding a means to cope with these children and help them with their difficulties is extremely important. We as parents and teachers need to become informed about research on ADD and various treatments and strategies available, and to understand and support each other in dealing with their problems.

3

Causes of ADD:

What do the Experts Suspect?

Light blond hair, pale skin and big blue eyes gave Terry an angelic look, and he talked earnestly about his desire to learn and "be good" in school. His eyes lit up and beamed his pleasure on being praised or otherwise rewarded when he managed to follow school rules or when he accomplished a learning task.

Yet it was evident early that he didn't attend well to lessons, that noise and movement bothered him, and that his reactions to frustration were quick and extreme. Difficulties in learning showed up early as well, and testing revealed him to have average ability, but his pattern of scores was suggestive of learning problems. Behavior problems, however, were most evident and were present beyond situations where he was having learning difficulty.

When met with frustration, Terry was anything but angelic as he threw over desks and other furniture, swore, and threw items at the teacher and other students. His impulsiveness, aggressiveness and general inability to follow rules got him into further difficulties with peers and teachers. At times he appeared spoiled and willful as he broke rules, then argued that he didn't like the rules so he shouldn't have to follow them. He couldn't seem to resist running and pushing to get to the head of a line, or calling out answers or other thoughts that came to mind. He was often in difficulty for hitting, kicking and otherwise attacking those he disagreed with or thought to be making fun of him or looking at him the wrong way. Behavior management programs were tried, but had little effect on his impulsive volatile behavior. As he entered his third year of school, he still hadn't learned to read.

He was then placed in a class with a low enrolment where behavior management techniques were continued. Importantly, it seemed, he was now placed on medication. With the medication and the smaller class, he settled somewhat, became more amenable to behavior management and began to learn to read.

In looking at Terry's history, it was found that he was born over a month prematurely and weighed less than four pounds at birth. The pregnancy had been a difficult one for his mother who had suffered nausea and bleeding throughout most of it. As a baby, Terry was unhappy, colicky, and sickly and required much care. He had pneumonia three times in his first year of life as well as numerous ear infections. In the preschool years, he developed asthma and other allergies and continued to have repeated bouts of respiratory infections after he entered school.

He had an older brother who presented no behavior problems at school, but because of learning problems had repeated a grade.

Factors as Causal or Associated with ADD

While Terry's case illustrates a number of factors experts have postulated might be causal or predisposing toward ADD, it also gives examples of other factors which, though not seen to be causal, are often associated with ADD. One of these is being male.

Obviously, being male does not cause hyperactivity, but it is generally accepted that if you are a boy your chances of having ADD are from four to nine times higher than if you happen to be a girl. The reason for this is not known. It is possible that a sex-linked genetic trait is involved or there may be other unknown reasons — the same reasons that boys are more prone to mental retardation and other psychological disorders.

However, it may turn out that ADD is largely under-diagnosed in girls and this particular statistic may change as more becomes known about the numbers of children — many of them girls — who have ADD without hyperactivity. Though ADD children without hyperactivity don't show excessive movement or the more disruptive behaviors, experts believe that they may have emotional, social and academic problems just as serious as other ADD children (Ingersoll 1988, 5).

Some authorities have also noted that there are three times as many blue-eyed or green-eyed blond children who have ADD as brown-eyed children with darker hair (Smith, 38; Gold, xxiv). While, according to some, the chances of having ADD increase if a child has blue or green eyes and blond hair, it is not clear how this relates to the proportion of blue or green-eyed blonds in a total population.

Having the particular learning problems often called learning disabilities or specific developmental disorder is not seen to cause ADD, but experts estimate that up to 20 percent of learning disabled students also have ADD (Barkley 1985, 169). Some believe that when children have both ADD and learning disabilities these two problems stem from a common cause.

Are the Parents to Blame?

In the case of Blair, another ADD child with behavior and learning problems, his mother had experienced learning and behavior problems when she was in school and still seemed very excitable. She showed a great deal of concern about Blair's experiences at school and had complained about some of the methods used to try and normalize his behavior. As well, she said she had trouble handling him at times, and there had been a divorce in Blair's young life.

From this information it could be concluded that Blair's problems stemmed from modelling on his mother's undesirable behavior; from being overprotected and spoiled (or not properly trained in self-control and following rules); or from emotional trauma resulting from the divorce and associated events.

In fact, this would be a common interpretation of the facts in Blair's case. That the parents or the home-life are the source of a child's difficult behavior is one of the most common misconceptions about ADD.

A Comparison to the Causes of Learning Disability

Twenty years ago little was known about children with learning disabilities. It was known that some children with a normal or higher intelligence level failed to learn as other children did and fell further and further behind in one or more areas of learning as they proceeded through school. The prevailing theory at the time was that if children of normal intelligence weren't learning in school it was because they lacked the proper motivation. The most likely source of their defective motivation was apparently the home. Because these children had been tested and were found to have the intellectual capabilities necessary to succeed in school, few thought to look inside the child or considered that there might be other problems that prevented success in school.

My university textbook had explained the necessity of motivating children, saying that a need or motive was the starting point for all learning and that the job of the teacher was to manage student motivation and thus encourage student learning. Some ways to instill beneficial motives were through tangible rewards (mostly gold stars in those days) and privileges, through approval from teacher, peers and family, and through encouraging the child to feel good inside about his accomplishments (intrinsic motivation — the best kind) (Sawrey and Telford 1958, 16). However, many young teachers learned that, do what they might, with some students they could not overcome the effects of a poor upbringing and the resulting poor motivation. They could lead a student to the fountain of knowledge, but they could not make him thirsty.

This is not to say that motivation is unimportant to learning — every teacher knows it is. There are obviously students who would learn better if their motivation was higher — and some of these are likely also learning disabled children. What this illustrates is that a theory or belief can be carried too far, and that if one accepts a theory, the facts can be made to fit it. It made perfect sense that these students were not learning because they didn't value the learning sufficiently. The types of avoidance behaviors such students developed in the face of their failure was more evidence of their lack of initiative.

It is now generally accepted that many students have perceptual or language handicaps, or what might be called learning disabilities (or specific developmental disorder), that make it very difficult for them to learn some subjects in a regular class with regular methods. Few still believe that the main source of such learning problems is the home situation or poor motivation.

We have a strong belief in our society that behavior is the result of experiences. We don't leave much room for the possibility that other strong influences may interact with experience to shape behavior. There are undoubtedly students who would pay attention and behave better in school if they had been trained differently by their parents or if the level of family stress were lower, but in many cases these are not the main factors in behavior and learning problems.

The View of Some Mental Health Professionals

To add to this, many of our mental health professionals to whom we look for guidance have a strong belief in the home as the major influence on child behavior. They seem to believe if parenting is good, the child will be good. They have often been trained this way and interpret what they see in much the same way as teachers used to interpret the behavior of learning disabled students. Some are still unaware of or discount the recent research on ADD.

When mental health professionals point to the home as the source of problem behavior in children, they often look for problems in the discipline or parenting procedures used with a child. As well, they may look for disturbed family dynamics or family stress, such as might be present if there had been a divorce or if a family member suffered from mental illness. It has been well-established in the literature of mental health professions that both of these types of factors can influence child behavior.

Study on the Causes of Behavior Problems

A study carried out by a group of psychologists a number of years ago illustrates how strongly teachers have been influenced by the belief that unwholesome behavior comes from unwholesome experiences. The psychologists randomly selected a number of students from the classes of a number of teachers. They made up imaginary psychological problems for each of the selected students. The psychologists then told the teachers about the imaginary disorders of their various students and asked the teachers if they knew of any family problems that would account for such problems in the students. In every case, the teachers were able to come up with parenting short-comings, family dysfunction or home stresses that would account for the student problems.

What this study illustrates best, perhaps, is that few parents are perfect and most families have some types of problems, and that if we are looking to the home for the cause of a problem, we are likely to find it.

If other family problems are not readily evident, we can always point to birth order as a possible cause of undesirable behavior. If a child is the oldest in the family, we can surmise, and probably find evidence to back us, that the parents expected too much of the child, and that they were inexperienced and used trial and error in child management. For a middle child, we might point out that the child had trouble finding a "place" in the family and that he didn't get as much attention as older and younger siblings. It is often easy to presume that a youngest child is spoiled; as he is overprotected by parents and older siblings alike.

The Situation in Homes of ADD Children

Often, one of these factors — either defective parenting or family stress — and frequently both, are found in the homes of ADD children. However, according to experts, these factors are never the cause of ADD. They frequently are the result of the difficulty the ADD child has presented in the family and they can worsen the problems of the ADD child. They may in some cases be largely irrelevant to the ADD problem. Put simply: though family and discipline problems can result from ADD in a child and can worsen ADD in a child, family problems or poor discipline never *cause* ADD in a child (Wender 1987, 27).

While it is common for others to believe that an ADD child is spoiled or undisciplined — just the opposite is more likely to be the case. Because of the frequent problems and the escalating misbehavior of the ADD child, his parents often show much higher levels of commands, discipline and negative interactions than is common in other child-parent situations (though they don't always do this in public as they may anticipate an extreme scene). While there are instances where parents wear-out or give up on trying to discipline an ADD child, much more frequently the misbehavior of the ADD child leads to a very high level of control reactions and prohibitions on the part of parents (Barkley 1985, 176). Thus, while it's common for observers to believe parents need to be taught to exert more control over their child, experts are of a different opinion.

Interestingly, when experts in ADD noticed the high control and command level shown by parents of ADD children, they at first wondered if the excessive control had caused the ADD behaviors (Barkley 1985, 176). Most experts now agree that such is not the case, but they do believe that extreme amounts of control exacerbate the child's problems. As a result, counselling efforts are often directed toward lowering negative controlling actions on the part of parents.

Evidence that parents' extreme control reactions are the result rather than the cause of ADD is shown in studies where ADD children are put on medication and their behavior becomes more acceptable (Barkley 1985, 176). The number of control and discipline reactions on the part of the parents decreases immediately as the behavior of the children improves (Barkley 1985, 176). It is also interesting to note that the same type of negative control patterns often develop between teachers and ADD students.

Evidence against the Family as a Cause of ADD

There are a number of other factors that experts point out when explaining that ADD is not caused by parenting or family problems. The first of these is the early presence of ADD symptoms. In many cases, these children show their difficult temperaments from the earliest days. Although not all ADD children are difficult babies, and some difficult babies do not turn out to have ADD, there is a clear relationship between fussy, restless, unpredictable behavior as a baby and the later presence of ADD.

For many ADD children there seems to be clear evidence that ADD may be genetically linked. Adoption studies have shown that, though separated at birth, full siblings of ADD children are twice as likely as half-siblings to have ADD. In fact, a study of identical twins showed that if one twin had ADD, chances were 100 percent that the other twin would also have it (Ingersoll 1988, 58). In any family with an ADD child, the chances are higher for other children in the family to have ADD as well, and for fathers and other close male relatives to report that they had similar problems as children. This is true whether or not the father or other relative has had contact with the ADD child. As well, other problems known to run in families such as alcoholism and depression have a higher incidence in the relatives of ADD children. These are the same disorders to which ADD children are susceptible as adolescents and adults (Ingersoll 1988, 58).

In many families of ADD children, there are other normal children in the family with no more problems than the average child. This is true in spite of the genetic connection and in spite of the fact that the presence of an ADD child often causes severe family stress — including problems for siblings.

Other problems often seen along with ADD give rise to the speculation that certain problems and ADD may have a common cause. Such problems include minor physical anomalies often seen in ADD children, the high incidence of learning disabilities compared to other children, the frequent illnesses during babyhood and, though not clinically significant, the higher number of abnormal EEGs and soft neurological signs seen in ADD children.

The Relative Effect of Child-Rearing Practices on ADD

Although child-rearing practices do not cause ADD, they may in some cases make its symptoms worse. The extreme control and negative interaction patterns that often develop in such families, and the high level of dominating behavior the ADD child and parents show toward each other cannot only make the family a very unhappy place to live, but can worsen the symptoms shown by the ADD child.

Because the severity of ADD physiological symptoms varies from child to child, it is often difficult to determine the part that biologic traits have played and the part family management or stresses has played. Some ADD children with a strong inborn component will have substantial problems no matter how they are raised or whether or not there are family difficulties. Others will have only minor problems unless family problems are substantial. Some such children do quite well until a major family problem arises.

It is difficult to see the part that physiological or environmental problems have played in an individual case of ADD; therefore, it is important to consider both physical or medical treatment and psychological treatment for each ADD child. Behavior management treatment is sometimes futile until the physical condition is corrected, and effective medical treatment can often be strengthened by psychological programs. For some children, specific educational interventions may be necessary. These issues will be discussed further in Chapters Six, Seven and Eight.

The Likelihood of Multiple Causes for ADD

If parents don't cause ADD in their children, what does? Most experts now agree that there are likely a number of different causes of ADD. Some cases seem to be related mostly to one single cause, while other cases seem to be caused by a variety of components contributing in different amounts to the problem. Russell A. Barkley, Ph.D., Chief of the Neuropsychology Section of the Medical College of Wisconsin, suggests that the causes of ADD may be likened to the causes of mental retardation in that many are biologic, some are environmental-social and some are a combination of both (Barkley 1985, 177).

Inborn Temperamental Traits as Causes

Scientists have now shown us what everybody's grandmother knew: babies are born with different dispositions.

Some babies are easygoing and placid from their earliest days, while others are more demanding and intense. Some settle easily into predictable routines of eating and sleeping, while others never seem to settle into regular habits.

A longitudinal study done in New York followed a large group of children from birth to late adolescence (Ingersoll 1988, 52). It found that right from birth, children exhibit distinct temperaments and these temperaments tend to be stable over the years. The 10 percent of children found to have difficult temperaments were also found to be particularly prone to developing later behavioral disturbances.

In some cases, it is thought that the difficult temperament seen in ADD is just an extreme version of the traits of restlessness, impulsivity, and inability to focus attention and that these traits are passed on genetically. Just as some people are taller than others, so are some more restless and impulsive than others. Unfortunately, those at the extreme end of the continuum for these traits have difficulty fitting into our schools and a society which demands self-control and sustained attention for success.

Eminent neurologist, Richard M. Restak, M.D., author of The New York Times best-seller, *The Brain,* has more recently written *The Mind,* which is the companion volume to the landmark PBS television series of the same name. In it he explains the components and functioning of the mind and various influences which determine differences in the minds of individuals and in their behavior. He describes a suspected genetic connection found in alcoholism (which, in turn, is connected to ADD) (Restak 1988, 123). Through studies of brain function, scientists have now found what they believe may be a genetic marker for alcoholism. Yet, what appears to be inherited is a genetic propensity or vulnerability to alcoholism rather than a genetic trait which *always* causes alcoholism. Other complex, interrelated biological and psychological factors which are not fully understood also seem to come into play. It is quite possible that similar factors are important in the outcome and degree of severity of ADD.

Environmental Causes

Some feel that harmful factors in a child's environment may at times cause ADD. It has long been known that some children who ingested lead (usually from chewing lead-base paint on cribs, etc.) developed hyperactivity (Wender 1987, 31). Now some studies have found that some children diagnosed as hyperactive who live in large cities may have mild, chronic lead poisoning. It is feared that these children may have developed lead poisoning leading to ADD from breathing fumes of automobiles as a result of living in heavily trafficked areas. It is not yet known how to accurately measure levels of lead in the body or how to determine what levels are detrimental to children. At present, most experts believe that lead poisoning is an unlikely cause of hyperactivity in most children.

Another suggested environmental cause is food or other substances to which a child might be sensitive. There are over 4,000 chemicals used in food processing today (Ingersoll 1988, 56). Some specialists feel that some of these may be responsible for ADD symptoms in some children. Dr. Benjamin Feingold, an allergist who popularized his additive-free Feingold diet, is a leading proponent of this theory. In his book, *Why Your Child is Hyperactive* (1975), he speculates that about half of the cases of hyperactivity are due to allergy-like reactions to food or chemical additives in food. Other specialists point to various natural foods they believe may cause allergic reactions and result in hyperactivity. Some suggest a child may be sensitive to fumes or lighting in the environment.

Another theory has been proposed by Dr. Lendon H. Smith in his book, *Improving Your Child's Behavior Chemistry* (1976). He suggests that hyperactivity and other behavior disorders may be due to hypoglycemia (low blood sugar), or to a lack of vitamins. He recommends dietary changes and vitamin and mineral supplements as a way to overcome the problem. Diet and supplements as a means to deal with hyperactivity will be discussed further in Chapter Six.

Trauma during Pregnancy or Birth

Another possible cause of the difficult temperaments of some babies and later ADD problems might be that something had gone wrong either during pregnancy (prenatal period) or during the birth process (perinatal period). It has been found that mothers of ADD children are more likely to report poor health during pregnancy than those of other children, and that a greater proportion of ADD children have mothers who were under twenty when the child was born. Richard M. Restak, M.D., in *The Mind* (1988), explains how damage caused by maternal drinking of alcohol has been linked to symptoms of ADD in children (Restak 1988, 41-42).

Heavy maternal smoking during pregnancy has also been found more often for hyperactive children (Ingersoll 1988, 55).

ADD children are more likely than others to have been firstborns and their mothers more frequently reported toxemia, an infection during which toxins circulate in the blood, or eclampsia, a condition involving coma or convulsions (Ingersoll 1988, 54). Children with ADD are more likely to have been born prematurely and to have had low birth weight (Wender 1987, 29) or to have been born postmaturely — at a gestational age of ten months or later (Ingersoll 1988, 55).

Hyperactive children are twice as likely to have had signs of fetal distress such as head injuries or other birth injuries, and the labor was more likely to have lasted longer than thirteen hours. They are also more likely to have had medical problems or physical malformations at birth (Ingersoll 1988, 55). It is possible that these problems during pregnancy and birth caused minor differences in the brains of ADD children which lead to ADD symptoms.

Brain Damage and Neurological Immaturity

Although experts say that brain damage can cause symptoms consistent with ADD, most children with definite brain damage do not develop ADD, and most ADD children do not show definite signs or a history consistent with brain damage (Barkley 1985, 175). Some experts have, however, proposed that neurological immaturity is sometimes responsible for ADD symptoms. They emphasize the fact that ADD children often appear like normal younger children and that the EEGs of some ADD children suggest an immaturity in the brain (Barkley 1985, 175). Soft neurological signs, such as gross motor or fine motor problems seen in some ADD children are also sometimes seen in nonhyperactive children, so their significance is not clear (Moghadam 1988, 21).

There is considerable evidence, nevertheless, that ADD may be the result of a malfunction of the frontal lobes of the brain. Such a malfunction could sometimes be the result of heredity or due to problems during pregnancy or during the birth process. In other cases, it could be caused by lead poisoning or sensitivities to food or chemicals and other toxins in the environment.

The frontal lobes of the brain are involved in regulating attention, activity level and emotions. When this part of the brain is damaged in laboratory monkeys, the monkeys become hyperactive, easily distracted and emotionally volatile — similar to the hyperactive child (Ingersoll 1988, 64). The frontal lobes also aid in the ability to plan ahead, another area in which ADD children are weak. People with known frontal lobe damage show similarity to ADD children in that they have trouble with planning ahead, controlling impulses and emotions, and following rules even though they are able to understand and repeat them. Thus, many experts believe that, though there may not be brain damage, a malfunction in the frontal lobes of ADD children is a likely cause of their symptoms.

Chemical Differences in the Brain

One possible cause of the individual differences in the function of the frontal part of the brain could be chemical differences in the brains of affected individuals. Experts believe such chemical differences likely account for the inborn temperamental differences seen in children (Wender 1987, 29).

In the case of genetic inheritance, children on the extreme end of the scale for activity level, impulsiveness, lack of ability to focus and concentrate, and low emotional control would be those who inherited too much or too little of certain brain chemicals. In other children, brain chemicals may have been within the normal range until some trauma during pregnancy or birth changed the chemical makeup. As well, malnutrition or toxins such as lead may affect these brain chemicals before or after birth.

The chemicals in the brain that transmit messages from nerve cell to nerve cell are called neurotransmitters. Experts believe that ADD may be caused by breakdowns or imbalances in neurotransmitter systems. When drugs are used in treatment of ADD, they are thought to correct this chemical imbalance and thus allow normal functioning of the brain and the individual (Ingersoll 1988, 60).

Drugs can influence these neurotransmitters in a variety of ways (Ingersoll 1988, 61). They may interfere with the production of certain neurotransmitters, resulting in a lower level of these messenger chemicals in the brain if this is what is needed. Other drugs may step-up the production of certain neurotransmitters, or may provide a substitute for natural neurotransmitters, thus providing more of specific neurotransmitters to the brain and allowing it to function more normally. This is believed to be the reason that drugs used in treatment of ADD seem to affect the basic reasoning powers of an individual and correct behavior in a profound way, rather than just masking symptoms.

Promising New Approaches to Brain Study

The new techniques of brain imaging, unlike traditional x-ray techniques, give a clear picture of brain structure (Ingersoll 1988, 62) and may prove useful in studying brain function in ADD children. The most familiar of these new techniques is the computerized tomography (CT) scan which uses x-rays to construct a vivid computerized image of the brain.

Other brain imaging techniques enable researchers to observe the brain while it is working by measuring blood flow to various sections of the brain. Radioactive substances are used as "tracers" to measure blood flow in different sections of the brain. Since patients are exposed to some radiation during the use of this technique, its use is greatly restricted.

However, this technique was used in Denmark to study a group of hyperactive children. Reduced blood flow to the frontal lobes of the brain was found in every hyperactive child examined. These children were then given Ritalin, a stimulant drug frequently administered in the treatment of ADD children. Increased blood flow in the frontal lobes of the brain was then seen in all the children (Ingersoll 1988, 63).

Another new brain imaging technique called the PET scan (positron emission tomography) is being used at the National Institute of Mental Health in Bethesda, Maryland, to look at brain functioning in hyperactive adults (Ingersoll 1988, 63). Using the PET scan, radioactive substances that emit positrons are used to trace glucose in the brain where it is used as fuel. Because the most active parts of the brain use the most glucose, scientists can see which parts of the brain are most active. It is still too early to know what this research will tell us about hyperactivity.

The Adoption Connection

Researchers estimate that as many as one in five adopted children have ADD. (Looking at the proportion of boys to girls diagnosed with ADD, it becomes evident that a great many adopted boys will have ADD.) In comparison, it is believed that about one in twenty children in general have ADD to varying degrees. Formerly, many of these adopted children had been diagnosed as having emotional problems stemming from the adoption rather than as having ADD (Ingersoll 1988, 59).

Though it is not known why there is such a high incidence of ADD in adopted children, it is known that many children put up for adoption are born to very young mothers — a factor related to ADD. Researchers have also found that among the biological parents and other blood relatives of adopted ADD children there is a higher than average proportion of ADD as well as related disorders such as depression and alcoholism (Ingersoll 1988, 59). On the other hand, among adoptive parents the incidence of these disorders is low because most adoptive parents have been carefully screened.

The Interplay between ADD and Life Experiences

A child with ADD initially shows a difficult temperament which is the result of his biological make-up. However, as he progresses through life, reactions of others to his unpleasantness and the frequent failure he experiences add to his problems. Because of his aggressiveness and disobedience, he will likely have parents and others angry with him a great deal of the time. This makes him feel rejected which often turns into further anger and aggressiveness on his part.

If parents in their desperation have used harsh punishments and name calling, these may significantly elevate his feelings of anger and lead to greater rebelliousness. Extreme punishment can lead to further psychological maladjustment as well, which is difficult to treat. A child who is already physically aggressive will become more so with repeated physical punishment used against him.

Peers will likely have shunned him because of his bossiness and his inability to stick with a game or activity. It is possible that peers will have provoked, taunted and teased him too because of his volatile temper and frequent tears. These children often feel desperately in need of friends, but have difficulty keeping them.

Once into school, the ADD child will have experienced much reprimanding and criticism because of his undesirable behavior. Even if he is bright and doesn't have any special learning difficulties, he will have a harder time learning than other children due to his inattentiveness, haste and inability to keep on task. By the time he gets very far in school he is likely to have experienced failure and criticism academically and may feel he is dumb.

The problems of ADD children often form a vicious cycle and become progressively worse as the self-esteem of the child lowers. The earlier treatment is begun, the more chance there is of effectively interrupting the cycle. Oftentimes treatment is rejected or delayed because it is known that ADD children sometimes outgrow their hyperactivity problems. Unfortunately, while some do outgrow these problems, even they are often left with lowered self-esteem, unhappy memories, and other problems secondary to the ADD that might have been at least partially prevented.

Conclusion

While there are no definite answers as to the cause of ADD in children, evidence definitely suggests that the cause is not faulty parenting or stresses in the home. These factors can, however, worsen ADD.

It is most probable that there are a variety of causes for ADD, and that in some cases the cause is singular, while in others more than one factor plays a part. Among the possible causes of ADD that have been put forth are inborn temperamental differences possibly resulting from genetic inheritance, or difficulties before or during the birth process that lead to differences in brain functioning. Another general cause might be injury from the environment which includes ingestion of toxic substances such as lead, sensitivities to food and food additives, and nutritional deficiencies.

Once ADD symptoms present themselves as difficult behaviors, they result in negative life experiences for the child. These patterns often snowball and set up a vicious cycle between the negative behavior on the part of the child and negative life experience for the child. In other words — the bad behavior of the child results in bad experiences for him which in turn worsen his behavior.

4

Testing and Diagnosis:

How is ADD Identified?

When Russell was adopted at three weeks of age, he was already a busy baby, reaching, touching, pulling, and putting everything he could into his mouth. At first his mother thought his frequent crying and fussiness were part of a settling in period, but as the weeks passed they continued. He cried often, day and night, and was difficult to comfort.

Unfortunately, his mother had read in a magazine that if an adopted baby cried a lot it might mean that the parent and baby were ill-matched and that, possibly, the baby should be removed from the home. Understandably, she was hesitant to complain too much to her doctor about the difficulty she was having.

As the weeks went by, Russell's crying and sleeplessness continued. One-half hour was a long daytime nap for him and he slept only two hours at a time during the night. His activity level continued to increase, and he squirmed and pushed against being held for very long. By three months, he was rolling around on the floor and starting to pull himself along.

A friend of his mother, who was a nurse at a local children's hospital, observing his high activity level and fussiness, suggested he might be hyperactive. Because he was a first baby, his mother had no clear idea of normal fussiness or activity level, but thought hyperactive was a drastic label, and that love and care would help Russell settle and become an easier child.

By the time he reached toddlerhood, she realized that considerable discipline would also be needed. He was into everything and had extreme tantrums when frustrated or thwarted. When he was three, his younger sister was adopted. Caring for another child, his mother now understood what a difficult baby Russell had been.

The presence of a new sibling in a home often causes a deterioration in the behavior of an older child. In a home with a hyperactive child, the adjustment is often more difficult, and continuing conflicts due to sibling rivalry are often more severe. This was the case in Russell's home. A new baby sister brought much more than just another child to care for. It brought the need for even more constant vigilance over Russell because of his continual pestering and aggressiveness toward his young sister.

By the time Russell was five, his mother was at her wit's end. She went to her family doctor asking for help either for Russell or herself, as she felt the stress of dealing with him was becoming too much for her. The family doctor, who had seen Russell several times previously, observed him in his office and concluded that he was very active and inattentive. He prescribed a trial on Ritalin, a stimulant medication often used with hyperactive children, to see if this would benefit Russell. Wisely, he suggested Russell see a pediatrician who was associated with a children's hospital and specialized in such disorders. Because Russell's mom was clearly distraught, he suggested she talk to a psychologist as well at the children's hospital.

On his first visit to the pediatrician, Russell was given a physical exam to rule out other possible physical causes for his behavior. Then Russell was asked to perform a number of physical exercises (such as hopping and balancing on one foot) to check for soft neurological signs and possible learning disabilities. The pediatrician observed Russell's distractibility, his quick answers, and his squirming and ticklishness even though he was now on a small dosage of Ritalin and, according to his mother, his behavior had improved somewhat. The doctor made notes on all his findings.

Still watching Russell out of the corner of his eye, he interviewed Russell's mother about his developmental history. What had he been like as a baby? How often had he been sick? With what? At what ages did he walk and talk, etc.? He asked questions about discipline methods used and about family problems and stresses. He asked her about the types of problems she was having with Russell in terms of his activity level, his impulsiveness, his distractibility, his interactions with his sister and other children, his compliance, and his reaction when he didn't get what he wanted. He agreed that Russell was hyperactive and suggested that the dosage of Ritalin be slowly increased to see if Russell's response would improve.

Before Russell's mother met with the psychologist, he contacted her by phone and asked if she and Russell's father would fill out some questionnaires that would be sent in the mail. She was also to take a questionnaire to Russell's kindergarten teacher for her to fill out concerning Russell's behavior at school. The home questionnaires consisted of rating scales on which the parents rated how often their child displayed certain behaviors, as well as some questions about troublesome behaviors and the parents' response to them. The school questionnaire was similar.

After this, Russell's mother met with the psychologist and talked about the stress she was experiencing. She set up an appointment for the psychologist to come into the home to observe Russell with the rest of the family (except for the dad who was at work). On the appointed day, the psychologist stayed for two to three hours interacting with Russell and observing him in his family setting.

He watched Russell at play with other children and interacting with his sister. He saw Russell's mother issue requests and commands and noted Russell's level of cooperation. He ate lunch with the family and played a board game with them, noting Russell's need to win and his short attention span. The psychologist met with both parents a few times, and with the mother a number of times until she was feeling more secure in her ability to accept and cope with Russell's behavior.

A few years later, Russell's family moved. A new doctor took Russell off the medication, believing that he should have outgrown the need for it. By the time Russell entered junior high school, he was having academic problems and home life had again become conflict ridden. His teachers became concerned about his low marks and his deteriorating attitude, and Russell was tested by the school psychologist. The psychologist checked his intellectual ability and achievement levels. He measured Russell's visual and listening skills. He also used questionnaires to determine emotional and social adjustment and to get a measure of Russell's self-esteem.

Though his native ability and scores on standardized achievement tests were for the most part high, Russell did poorly on some tests that depended on good concentration and freedom from distractibility. He also showed weaknesses in fine motor speed and control (important to printing and handwriting), and in some listening skills necessary to success in school (and also dependent on good concentration). Predictably, he showed problems in emotional and social adjustment and his self-esteem was low.

The psychologist met with his parents and explained some of his findings. He believed Russell's distractibility and emotional problems to be the main factors interfering with his school achievement. The psychologist also reported to Russell's teachers and suggested several strategies such as giving oral or multiple choice tests to compensate for Russell's difficulty with writing quickly and legibly. These strategies, he suggested, might help Russell achieve closer to his ability level.

During the assessment, the psychologist also noted that in a few parts of some listening tests Russell remembered nothing at all. The psychologist felt that the possibility of a subtle seizure disorder causing memory blanks should be investigated. Russell, now thirteen, went to a neurologist and was given an EEG. The neurologist also had him do a number of coordination and balancing tasks similar to those given by the pediatrician when Russell was five. He sent his findings to Russell's family doctor who put Russell back on stimulant medication.

The neurologist also showed the EEG and other test results to both Russell and his mother. The EEG, he explained, was suggestive of a subtle seizure disorder, but was not conclusive. Since his mother could not recall any instances of staring spells or memory loss, it was decided not to put him on medication for seizures. The EEG, the neurologist said, was also similar to that often found in ADD children.

Initial Suspicions of a Parent or Teacher

Often parents will have noted problems in the ADD child some years before the child is taken for diagnosis. However, if the child is a first child or if there is more than one hyperactive child in the family, parents may not realize the extreme nature of their child's behavior. They may think that all families have the same degree of difficulty with their children or, more commonly, think they are doing something wrong that has caused the behavior. When the child is younger, they may think his behavior will improve as he gets older, as this is true for the conduct of many children as they graduate from their "terrible twos."

When an ADD child enters school he is often seen by teachers to be immature and is given the benefit of the doubt that he will improve as he gets used to the demands of school. Academic problems may not surface in the first few grades where activities change more often, lessons are more "hands-on," and assignments are simpler and require less writing, organization and sustained attention.

When ADD children are finally referred for help it is usually because of their lack of academic achievement or because of behavior problems. It is often not realized that they have problems in focusing and concentration or with impulsivity. It may be noticed that they are very active, but it may not be recognized that, often, it is an inability to curb activity that gets them into trouble. When students are referred for help because of learning or behavior problems, the help they are given may focus on remediating weak skills or dealing with the undesirable behavior — still not recognizing the underlying ADD.

Reasons ADD is Underdiagnosed

According to experts in the field, ADD is still greatly underdiagnosed for a number of reasons. There are some who still believe it doesn't exist and others who think it is a minor problem easily dealt with if one has the right attitude. Some still adhere to the notion that ADD children must move a lot in all situations. They don't realize that these children can at times — particularly with less familiar people, surroundings and activities — be quite still and focused.

Especially likely to be missed are those children whose problems are attentional without excess movement. As mentioned before, many of these are girls, and though they may have problems with their learning, with their peers and with their self-concept as serious as those of the more active ADD child, they are not often diagnosed.

There is still a great deal of disagreement among experts as to all the symptoms that constitute ADD and the degree of severity that is significant. Even among experts there is some difference of opinion as to which particular children should be diagnosed as ADD. Among parents and teachers there is an even greater variance of opinion.

Another reason some children are missed is because parents are hesitant to complain about problems they may be having with a child or to take him to a specialist for fear of receiving criticism instead of help. Most parents who have read at all in the area of parenting are aware of the general view that problem children are the result of faulty parenting. Already feeling stress, guilt and self-criticism, they may be hesitant to invite more criticism.

The Relationship of ADD to Conduct Disorders

One of the areas where there is disagreement among experts is in distinguishing ADD from a group of disorders called conduct disorders of childhood. Some of the aggressive and antisocial problems seen in some ADD children are also seen in conduct disorders. Some believe that ADD is simply a subgroup of conduct disorders (Barkley 1985, 181).

Others maintain that while the two groups of disorders have many overlapping features, the central features of ADD are poor attention, poor impulse control, and difficulty following rules. Conduct disorders are seen to be principally characterized by persistent and repetitive aggression and antisocial behaviors against others and their property, with little regard for the welfare of others (Barkley 1985, 181). This book refers to the aggression and antisocial behavior sometimes seen in ADD children, but which is not as severe or persistent as that generally described under conduct disorders.

Who is Qualified to Diagnose ADD?

ADD is a medical and psychological diagnosis and is generally made by a psychiatrist, psychologist, neurologist, pediatrician or other medical doctor. Public health nurses, mental health and social workers, teachers and others may be aware of the diagnostic criteria. These criteria generally compare the frequency and quality of behavior of a given child to that of a group of his peers. In other words, they ask if certain behaviors are seen a lot more and with a greater severity in a given child than in other children his age.

Teachers who are aware of the diagnostic criteria for ADD may have a particular advantage for picking out children with ADD, as they see and interact with large numbers of children every day. If they have in previous years had in their classes a number of children identified as ADD, this may be an advantage as well — although it can be a disadvantage if they believe any one child is "typically" ADD and compare others to him. It is also very likely that most teachers will have taught a number of ADD children who were never diagnosed as such and they should keep this in mind.

While many teachers may be able to pick out ADD children, they are not qualified to make a medical or psychological diagnosis or recommend treatment. Depending on established procedure, they may talk to the school counsellor or psychologist and have him test the child (with parental permission) and/or confer with parents about the behavioral or academic problems and possible avenues to investigate.

Alternately, they may talk to the child's parents about the types of problems they see the child having in school and suggest the child be examined by a psychiatrist, pediatrician, or other qualified professional to determine if these specialists can offer help for the school difficulties. As well, they may recommend reading in the area of ADD if parents show interest.

Teachers should remember in talking to parents that, as has been mentioned, to many people attention deficit disorder is a strong label and there is a great deal of misunderstanding about what it means. There may be reasons other than ADD for restless, inattentive, or disruptive behaviors, especially if the behaviors have not been long term. It is best to concentrate on describing the kinds of behaviors and academic problems the child is displaying and suggest the parent talk to the school psychologist or investigate other avenues. Either way, both a medical and psychological evaluation should be aimed for.

A parent's best bet in seeking evaluation is to first become as informed as possible about ADD, because, as experts point out, some doctors, psychologists or other mental health workers may not be aware of, or open to all the current knowledge about ADD. Once parents are aware of current information and research on ADD, there are a number of avenues they can investigate.

Dr. Paul Wender, professor of psychiatry and director of psychiatric research at University of Utah Medical Center, suggests that a child psychiatrist, a child neurologist or a pediatrician is likely to be most familiar with ADD. He explains that all physicians are not equally qualified in diagnosing and treating ADD, and more than one medical opinion may need to be sought in the search for a physician familiar with the full range of childhood physical and emotional problems including ADD (Wender 1987, 142). He states that not all physicians use medication in the treatment of ADD. Some avoid it routinely (Wender 1987, 143). As well, he cautions against seeing only a psychologist or social worker who may not be familiar with current medical research and treatment and cannot prescribe medicine if this is needed (Wender 1987, 141). While psychologists and social workers may be very helpful in dealing with psychological and family problems associated with ADD, some may recommend only counselling or behavior management programs and not suggest a medical opinion be sought.

Instruments and Techniques Used in Diagnosing ADD

Many of the tests and techniques used in diagnosing ADD were illustrated in Russell's story which introduced this chapter. A psychiatrist, neurologist, pediatrician or family physician will generally start with a medical examination to rule out physical causes for behaviors. He may also ask questions about stresses and problems in the home to determine how these might be affecting the child. (Remember, too, sometimes stress to a child can cause symptoms that are in some ways similar to ADD.)

During this time he will likely be observing the child's behavior. Even if the child behaves like a perfect angel in the office, as is sometimes the case, the doctor will likely be aware that this isn't necessarily typical of his behavior at other times. He may talk to and interact with the child to get an idea of his language and thinking style. To check for coordination and balance problems, he may have the child do a variety of physical tasks such as quickly following the doctor's finger with the child's finger and hopping on one foot.

The doctor will interview parents about the developmental history of the child: when he crawled, walked, talked, and the types of illnesses or problems such as stuttering he may have had. He will ask about sleep habits, reaction to change, and how he gets along with his siblings and playmates. He may ask questions and/or have parents fill out questionnaires or checklists based on ADD symptom lists.

One well known source of symptoms is the *Diagnostic and Statistical Manual* published by the American Psychiatric Association. This manual tries to standardize diagnostic practices among psychiatrists, psychologists and others who deal with psychiatric disorders. The third edition, which was revised in 1987, provides the following guidelines for diagnosing ADHD (attention deficit hyperactivity disorder) and states that a criterion is met only if the behavior is considerably more frequent than that seen in most people of the same mental age.

A. A disturbance of six months or more, during which at least eight of the following behaviors are present:

1. Often fidgets with hands or feet or squirms in seat (in adolescents may be limited to subjective feelings of restlessness).
2. Has difficulty remaining seated when required to do so.
3. Is easily distracted by extraneous stimuli.
4. Has difficulty awaiting turn in games or group situations.
5. Often blurts out answers to questions before they have been completed.
6. Has difficulty following through on instructions from others (not due to oppositional behavior or failure of comprehension); for example, fails to finish chores.
7. Has difficulty sustaining attention in tasks or play activities.
8. Often shifts from one uncompleted activity to another.
9. Has difficulty playing quietly.
10. Often talks excessively.
11. Often interrupts or intrudes on others; for example, butts into other children's games.
12. Often doesn't seem to listen to what is being said to him or her.
13. Often loses things necessary for tasks or activities at school or at home (for example, toys, pencils, books, assignments).
14. Often engages in physically dangerous activities without considering possible consequences (not for the purpose of thrill seeking); for example, runs into street without looking.

B. Onset before age of seven.

You will note that this particular list does not refer directly to the difficulty many ADD children have following rules, their oppositional and disobedient behavior, or the aggressive, bossy side often seen in relation to their peers. Some experts believe these categories should be added to these guidelines as they are so prevalent in ADD children. It has been found, in fact, that the

most disturbing symptom and the one most frequently responsible for the referral of these children to mental health clinics is
their obstinate, resistant behavior (Wender 1987,19). Many checklists and guidelines used in diagnosing ADD list these problem
areas as well.

In addition to questioning parents and/or having them fill out
questionnaires about the above areas, the doctor will often send
checklists for a teacher or daycare worker to fill out if relevant. If
the parents and the doctor agree that a trial period of medication
is warranted, he may ask them and/or the teacher to fill out such
checklists on a regular basis to help determine the effectiveness
of the treatment and the progress of the child.

Unless there are indications that the child may have a
neurological disease such as epilepsy, the doctor will not likely
order a neurological examination. EEGs and other such instruments, though sometimes showing irregularities for ADD
children, are not generally seen as useful in diagnosing ADD or
in determining treatment for children with ADD symptoms
(Wender 1987, 146).

If the child has not already had an individual psychologi-
cal/academic evaluation, the doctor may refer him to a
psychologist for one. Such an evaluation is often available
through the school system. The doctor may also recommend
family counselling or individual counselling for parents or the
child to help deal with stresses that are often present.

A psychologist will likely give the child an individual intelligence test to determine his native ability level and relative
strengths and weaknesses in a number of areas important to
success in school. He will also probably administer achievement
tests which estimate the child's present level of functioning in
areas such as reading and arithmetic. He may ask permission to
talk to teachers and look at school records to determine present
and past achievement levels in various subject areas.

From these tests and other information, a psychologist will
often be able to see the degree to which a child is underachieving
and if there are specific developmental disorders (learning disabilities) present. He may also get an idea of the child's distractibility, impulsivity, and fine motor coordination (necessary to
writing) by the scores on various subtests and the way the child
handles various tasks on these tests.

The psychologist may also use tests which check perception
(various vision and listening skills) and language development

and processing skills. He will most likely want to assess emotional and social adjustment as well as self-concept (how the child sees himself) and self-esteem (how the child feels about himself). In addition to completing various checklists and questionnaires with the child, he may ask the child about how he is doing in school, how he gets along with his agemates and how things are going at home with his parents and family. Some psychologists may want to come into the home to observe the child interacting with the family, particularly if there appears to be a need for family counselling.

Possible drawbacks of having an assessment done by a school psychologist may be in the degree to which the testing procedures are explained to parents as well as the amount and precision of results shared with them. There are still some jurisdictions where test scores and complete student files are not shared with parents. The exact nature of the tests, as well as the extent and form in which results will be communicated, may be something worth checking previous to allowing a child to be tested.

Conclusion

A variety of professionals may be involved in the diagnosis of ADD in a child. These include psychiatrists, neurologists, pediatricians, family doctors, psychologists, social workers, nurses and teachers. Those best qualified to look at all diagnostic and treatment options are generally a medical doctor or a psychologist: both of these should have experience and expertise in the area of ADD.

These practitioners generally use a variety of methods to determine whether a child has ADD. These include, physical examination of the child, an interview with parents as to the child's developmental history, observation of the child, and questions about home problems and stresses. Also, some practitioners will employ physical tests to check balance and coordination; checklists and questionnaires focusing on ADD symptoms; intelligence and achievement tests and records; perceptual and language tests; and psychological tests that measure social/emotional adjustment.

Before seeking evaluation of a child for ADD, it is advisable for parents to read current information about causes, diagnosis and treatment, so they will be aware of the various possibilities. Both a medical and psychological evaluation should be sought, and it may be necessary to seek more than one opinion in some areas before one finds a practitioner familiar with and open to all diagnostic and treatment procedures. Appendix A contains a check-list that parents who suspect their child may have ADD can use when seeking professionals most qualified to diagnose and treat ADD.

Viewpoints of Students,
Parents and Teachers:

Can These be Reconciled?

Ben was excited. Two friends had asked him to go bike riding after school. The teacher heard the three of them finalizing plans as they came in from recess. The other two settled to listen to the lesson, but Ben couldn't seem to contain himself. Not only was he calling out answers, but smart remarks as well, which often enough got their intended rise out of other students. Ben was sent out of the room until the listening part of the lesson was over.

When the class began a worksheet, Ben was allowed to return. The teacher explained the information he would need for the sheet and showed him how to do it. This was nothing out of the ordinary, as she often went over instructions with him when he failed to pick them up during class instruction.

Ben did the first two problems, then began to play with his pencil, catapulting it down the aisle. When corrected, he recovered his pencil and did a couple more problems, but was soon seen and heard to be searching the untidiness of his desk — this for a different pencil he told the enquiring teacher.

At five minutes to dismissal time, the few students not finished the assignment were urged to hurry. At this point Ben decided to get to work. He finished his worksheet on time, but most of what was legible was wrong. The teacher, exasperated, handed him a new worksheet with instructions to work more carefully and neatly.

Ben broke into tears, insisting vigorously he couldn't stay after class because he had plans to ride bikes with his friends. The teacher was adamant. Ben broke his pencil in two, slammed his fist on his desk, and began work. Finished in twenty minutes, he threw the paper on the teacher's desk and stamped from the room, his parting words, "I hate this school, and I'm never coming back."

When Ben arrived home he was still storming. He slammed open the door, broke into tears, and told his mother that the teacher wouldn't let him out on time so he could ride bikes with his friends. His mother, knowing that an invitation to play with others was uncommon for Ben, understood his grief.

She asked him why he wasn't let out. Ben grumbled that the teacher made him do his work over, even though he'd done it once. When questioned further he admitted that there were a few errors, "But not that many," he insisted, and, anyway, how did the teacher expect him to get the work right when he was out of the room while she was explaining it? Nothing was said about the individual instructions, or the untidiness of the work. Why was he out of the room? Because the teacher had it in for him. He just made a joke, and then she sent him out. She didn't like him anyway. He was always getting into trouble with her when he didn't even do anything.

When his mother suggested he look for his friends or try to catch up with them, Ben replied it was no use, they were already gone and he would never find them. He stamped into his room and could be heard crying and muttering about the mean teacher as he banged toys around.

In this situation, child, teacher and parent all felt frustrated and helpless in terms of knowing how to deal with or solve the problems.

The Student's Point of View

Many hyperactive children begin school enthusiastic and full of fun. They soon find out, however, that their undirected exuberance is not appreciated. They have difficulty organizing themselves and listening and following directions, but they don't understand this. They only know that they fail to please the teacher. Before long, they are having trouble academically and with their peers as well. It is no wonder that most don't like school.

academic problems

The short attention span of ADD children interferes with their hearing of lessons and instructions. They can't selectively focus their attention on one thing for very long. They can't tune out other stimuli, so anything that they can hear or see might draw their attention. As well, they can be internally distracted — caught up by their own racing thoughts. Consequently, they are often in trouble with the teacher for not paying attention.

The more potential distractions in a room, the more problems these students have. They may have particular difficulty if there is a lot of noise or movement. If there are other children causing distractions, they will be drawn to this rather than a lesson. For many of them, the subjects taught at school have little inherent interest. Many would rather learn about monsters, war heroes, weapons and dirt bikes. While they may not be much different from some other children in this respect, they have greater difficulty attending when interest is low.

They sometimes get the general idea of instructions or a concept, but miss important details. Yet, they don't know that they are missing important information until they have done something entirely wrong or are in the middle of a project. When they ask for redirection, they are often given a lecture on listening more carefully the first time.

Though they have been told they should listen more carefully, these children don't seem able to make themselves pay attention for very long. Attending and keeping their thoughts moving at a teacher's pace can be extremely tedious for them. The discomfort such children describe in trying to keep "on track" can be likened to the feelings we might have if we had to drive fifty miles at five miles per hour — keeping our mind on the road at all times. It probably wouldn't take long for us to start feeling bored and restless. Imagine what it would be like to spend several hours each day feeling like that.

These students have similar difficulties attending to written work for very long. They often have difficulty directing their attention to get started. Once started, and having done one or two problems of a certain kind or part of a report, they become very uncomfortable with the repetition and the tedium of keeping their mind focused on one thing.

They may have a perfect understanding of how to do problems or know all the ideas necessary to complete a report, but have trouble with the sustained attention and organizational skills necessary to get the ideas down on paper. These students will do much better on multiple choice or short answer tests than on those requiring longer, organized answers.

The result of their inability to keep their minds on lessons and focus their attention on assignments is usually considerable underachievement compared to their ability level. If they have specific learning disabilities their problems will be worse. As mentioned, they may have a good understanding of material, yet never put it down on paper. In other cases, they will have missed important concepts and details due to their inattention.

Many times their problems will be cumulative. Because they have missed important information, they don't understand new ideas. As they proceed through school, they get further and further behind. To add to this, as they progress to higher grades, the need for organization and sustained attention in completing assignments becomes greater, and what they produce will show even less of what they know.

There is a certain frustration inherent in knowing something or how to do something, but not being able to show it. As well, for the ADD student there is the demoralization of failure — of not doing as well as peers — of being called a dummy. Because of their low frustration tolerance, they give up easily which makes failure even more certain. Failure is particularly demoralizing for those ADD children who have a compelling need to win and to be the best.

On top of this, ADD children suffer the discomfort of staying relatively still — of not being able to satisfy strong urges to get up and move around. The tapping, rocking on chairs, poking others, going unnecessarily to the pencil sharpener and other activities they engage in, often get them into trouble both with peers and adults.

relationships with teachers

Much of the attention ADD children receive from teachers relative to their work will be negative, because what they are doing is negative in terms of their school progress. They aren't paying attention, they aren't settling down to work, and they're giving up as soon as they encounter minor difficulty. They are also likely doing other things that invite criticism — things like bothering others, calling out answers, and causing other disruptions to the smooth running of a class. Teachers try to find positive things to comment on for all students, but in some cases it can be hard.

relationships with peers

As mentioned earlier, relationships with peers are likely to be stormy. Playmates object to being bossed and to the poor sportsmanship ADD children often display. They sometimes resent the disruptions in school and laugh "at" rather than "with" these children, further hurting their feelings. Peers soon learn that they can get a strong reaction if they tease these children, and they have ample "ammunition" to use against them in terms of their poor academic showing, their disruptive displays, and the trouble they get into with teachers.

If an ADD child has problems in coordination, he may make a poor showing at sports. He may be the last chosen for informal teams and during school physical activities, and may do poorly on neighborhood teams. This adds another area of failure to his life and another situation where he may be shunned by others.

relationships with neighbors

Parents of playmates are often unimpressed by some of the ADD child's behavior. They may see him as spoiled or as just bad. Some may discourage their child from playing with him or may even forbid him to come into their house. When he does visit in the neighborhood or when he is in public places, the ADD child oftentimes finds yet more adults who offer disapproval. He is often left out of neighborhood gatherings and parties, too, either because his peers don't want him or their parents discourage asking him.

relationships at home

Long before he went to school, the ADD child was likely involved in much conflict at home. While his parents may have a better understanding of the difficulty he has in behaving as others expect, they will also have spent many more hours trying to discipline him and will most likely have lost patience with him at least some of the time. Because of the familiarity of home territory, the child's forgetting of rules and his disobedience may be greater here than at school. Regardless, he will be the object of much disapproval for his behavior at home as well as at school.

The ADD child will likely have the same kind of problems in getting along with brothers and sisters as with friends. Brothers and sisters may be embarassed by his behavior at school and may tease and censure him. Because his brothers and sisters get in less trouble than he does, he will see them as being favored by his parents. Sibling rivalry will be more extreme than in most families, and the ADD child will usually feel he is the loser.

lowered self-esteem

More negative commands, punishment, disapproval, teasing and blame comes the way of the ADD child than for most. He is also faced with more failure in school, in the family, in the neighborhood, and with peers. Consequently, as he gets older his self-esteem lowers.

He is hurt by the rejection and teasing of peers and often feels "different" from them. His failure in school and the high degree of disapproval and criticism he receives makes him feel dumb, bad and unlovable. These are not entirely irrational feelings, but rather are based on the facts. He is failing in every important area of his life, he gets constant criticism, and many don't like him. Why doesn't he take the easy route out and improve his behavior?

a bad attitude or an inability?

Is ADD an attitude toward one's own behavior, or an inability to control one's own behavior? Is the ADD child just stubborn and uncaring about pleasing others, or can he not control his behavior even though motivated to do so? Although the ability to control one's behavior and one's attitude about it are, obviously, intrinsically meshed, we can look at what these children say and do in an attempt to estimate the source of their problems.

Terry, from Chapter Three, when not in the heat of the moment, seemed unhappy with his misbehavior and genuinely motivated to behave well. He would say he wanted to "be good" and he clearly wanted the rewards offered for proper conduct. Yet when he was presented with temptation, felt an urge to do something, or became frustrated, he could only see his own desires. He was heedless of other's feelings, belligerent and determined to have what he wanted.

I remember many times with my son in his preschool years. He would be beside himself in his anguish over the fact I'd sent his friends home because of his aggression toward them. I would explain to him each time that if he couldn't play nicely, his friends couldn't stay. He would sob and sob, saying over and over that he was trying to be nice, but that he couldn't. Yet, when friends came again his poor conduct seemed flagrant. We would go through the whole scene again. Though he desperately wanted playmates, he never seemed to learn.

I remember one young girl who was frequently in trouble for calling out and for her remarks and swearing at other children. When I watched her, sometimes she literally seemed to be trying to catch the words as they came out. She would clap her hand over her mouth, but was always too late. Sometimes when I showed her something she had done wrong in her work, she would insist, "But it is right." She seemed to have a very strong need for her work to be right because she didn't want to correct it. However, in mid-sentence it seemed to come to her that she shouldn't argue with the teacher and her voice would fade to a whisper.

One young ADD teen as a preschooler had been quite aggressive physically, but by school-age had become more verbally aggressive, calling names or shouting when he didn't get his way. As a teen, when frustrated or wanting his own way, he still lost control of himself into verbal tantrums, punctuated by slamming doors and pounding his fist on the wall or a table. He occassionally, when in a spat with his younger brother, pushed or slapped him. After four months on medication this young teen's behavior had improved greatly, and he seemed much happier. However, in talking to a psychologist doing an educational assessment with him, he confided that he still worried that he might sometime lose control and make a fool of himself or seriously hurt someone. Unlike most ADD children (even when they are on medication), he was fairly self-aware, perhaps because he was also very bright.

I spoke in Chapter Three of watching learning disabled students at school, wondering why they would choose not to learn if they had a choice, because the rewards for learning were so high. I watched other students too — the ones who seemed eager to please in many ways, yet were always in trouble. I used to wonder, in particular, why they would do so many things to alienate their peers when they seemed to want friends so badly. Many experts now believe that if the ADD child could please others he would. It is not, they say, the child's will causing the bad behavior, but the ADD condition causing it (Moghadam 1988, 71; Ingersoll 1988, 120). They believe a belligerent or flippant attitude may either cover or be a result of their disability.

Nevertheless, these children often appear to have some control, especially as they get older. In some situations, at some times, they do seem to be able to control their behavior, so it seems that if they try they can behave acceptably. The fact is, many of them are moody and are believed to be at the mercy of their mood swings so that some days they have more control than others. Most of us have experienced days when, not feeling up to par, we are irritated by small matters or over-react to small incidents or the actions of others. This happens in spite of the fact that we as adults have a wide background of experience and have more ability to reflect on the appropriateness of our feelings. It seems probable that ADD children are in the grip of mood swings and are behaving in accordance with their feelings.

Adults who are clinically depressed often have pervasive feelings of sadness and hopelessness. Explaining to them that they have much to be happy about and that their life situation is no worse than that of many optimistic people may actually make them feel worse because they know they should feel happy, but they don't. It's as if they see the world through grey-colored lenses and explaining to them that they have these lenses does not change their view of the world. They may know it should look different, but it doesn't.

Hyperactive children at times seem to be wearing red-hot lenses which cause an exaggerated response to stimuli such as someone staring at them or noise and confusion — things which don't much bother the rest of us. At other times, their lenses seem to be exceedingly egocentric and seem to transform their desires into dire necessities. They seem to have such a strong need for having their way that to get it they will do things which are clearly not in their self-interest.

Whether it is the result of a bad attitude, or an inability to act in accordance with a good attitude, or a fluctuation from one to the other, these children have great difficulty controlling their behavior. Still, they want and need approval and rewards as much as any other child: often as they get older and their self-esteem lowers they crave approval more (although they may hide this).

These children, unable to see their part in problems, and lacking control over their attitudes and actions, blame others for their difficulties. They often complain, "It's not fair," or, "But I didn't do anything." They believe friends are being unfair and mean when they won't play. When they are reprimanded, they feel parents and teachers don't like them and have it in for them. As they get older, when called by an adult, they may reply in a defeated voice "What did I do now?" They expect to be blamed, still unfairly, for anything that has gone wrong.

An interesting study sheds some light on the perceptions and feelings of these children (Ingersoll 1988, 164). A group of elementary school students were given some fictional situations and asked to interpret them. One situation depicted restless, disruptive behavior of the type often seen in ADD children.

ADD children and non-ADD children differed markedly in how they saw the cause of this fictional misbehavior and the reasons for the teacher's negative reactions to it. Non-ADD children saw the character as being able to control his behavior. They said the teacher would react negatively with reprimands or punishment, and that was what she was supposed to do — it was her job.

ADD children, on the other hand, believed the character could not control the hyperactive-type behavior. They, too, believed the teacher would react negatively with reprimands or punishment, but they believed she reacted like this because she personally disliked the student or thought him to be a "bad boy."

This indicates that ADD children do not believe they are in control of their behavior, and that they think others shun and punish them because they don't like them. (It is unfair, after all, to punish someone for something they can't help.) If they can't control their behavior, then they have no choice but to receive blame and criticism. In this light their defensive behavior and later defeatist attitude make sense.

The Teacher's Point of View

An ADD child is the source of much frustration for a teacher. Not only does he make the teacher's job more difficult, but he threatens the teacher's self-esteem. He also affects the progress of other students and has a bad effect on classroom atmosphere.

excess time and attention spent on the ADD child

One of the things a teacher never has enough of is time — and the ADD student takes more of this precious commodity than seems fair. Not only does he require extra instruction and help because of his poor listening skills, but he may require frequent monitoring to keep him going on a task. There is also extra time required in disciplining him and in trying to gain his cooperation by talking with him and reinforcing any good behaviors he displays.

At the same time, the teacher will be attempting to get around to the other twenty-five to thirty-five students to help them with their problems. The time spent on the ADD child may seem especially unfair to other children with handicaps. There may in the classroom be children of low ability or with learning problems, children for whom English is a second language, or those with physical handicaps. Partly because the ADD child's problems seem willful, and partly because he demands attention rather than waits quietly for his turn, a teacher may find it hard not to resent the excessive amount of time spent on one child.

The ADD student may also add to time a teacher must spend preparing as he tries to work out strategies to keep this student interested and, sometimes, prepares special work for him. Teachers are often pressed for time to get all marking, classroom administration duties and preparation done, and this extra burden can be stressful.

teacher stress in dealing with disruptive and aggressive behavior

Added to the stress of never enough time and trying to keep programs on schedule is the stress of dealing with the behavior of the ADD child. The frequent attention the ADD child demands and the conflict that arises in disciplining him can be extremely wearing on stamina and nerves as can his unpredictability — never knowing when he's going to "blow."

Regularly, the teacher must deal with his outbursts, his complaints and demands, and his aggressive behavior toward other students. For some ADD students there will be the fear that they may seriously hurt another student during one of their fits of anger. Not surprisingly, on lists of job-related stresses of teachers, discipline problems are near the top. The teacher may also feel that the child doesn't like her, and her self-esteem as a teacher may be threatened. A teacher's self-esteem is generally tied to students liking her at least reasonably well and to feeling she is teaching effectively and is in control of the learning situation — all of which are in jeopardy with the ADD child.

In his book, *Teacher Burnout and What to do About it*, Stephen Truch, Ph.D., cites a study done in San Diego in which 77 percent of teachers surveyed reported physical symptoms of stress (such as fatigue and depression) occurring much of the time. Teaching is becoming a progressively more stressful profession as demands on teacher time, and the multitude of student and other problems with which a teacher must deal increases while the teacher remains vulnerable to criticism and evaluation from a variety of avenues. The ADD child may be another source of stress on an already overburdened teacher.

negative classroom atmosphere

Just as ADD children often bring out negative controlling patterns in parents, so do they in teachers. Studies have found that teachers give more commands, punishments and other punitive reactions to ADD children than to others. Not only this, in classrooms having an ADD child, the teacher gives more negative feedback to other children as well (Ingersoll 1988, 162). The presence of an ADD child seems to negatively affect the whole class atmosphere. Teachers are aware of class atmosphere and value a positive climate both for themselves and other students. They have often noted how the absence for the day of one ADD child can have a profound positive effect on the whole class and on the way they feel at the end of the day.

Besides the strain of dealing with the ADD child's behavior while trying to teach and direct the rest of the class, the teacher may fear that such behavior will have a bad influence on the rest of the class. Some students laugh at the antics of the ADD child, while others take advantage of the distraction of the teacher to talk to friends or otherwise waste time. At times, the teacher may fear that he will lose control of the class.

Understandably, he may be anxious about this and such anxiety may result in further adverse circumstances. Research done in a lab school looking at teachers and anxiety found that when teachers become anxious they become more tense, more demanding, less patient, less humorous, less organized, less confident and deal out more punishment (Ingersoll 1988, 162). Teachers are usually aware of this strain or anxiety, and usually percieve the resulting measures as necessary to keeping on top of the ADD child and in control of the class. Still, they are not pleased with the strict and often negative classroom atmosphere that ensues.

concern with the ADD child

Because a teacher can often see the good side of an ADD child, as well as the problems, she will often have taken a special interest in the child and tried to help him — sometimes to little avail. Knowing that she is dealing with a basically "good kid," a teacher will regret (and may feel guilty) about her inability to reach him. She may also feel concern about the future for this child who is such a problem.

degree of teacher difficulty

Individual teachers will, obviously, have different degrees of difficulty with any specific ADD child. Part of this will be due to the "match" between teacher and child. Most children like and get along better with some teachers than others. For the ADD child, however, this "match" factor may be critical. He may get along and work for one teacher quite well, whereas with another teacher, for reasons that seem related to the personalities of both the child and the teacher, he may dig in his heels and become very stubborn and difficult.

Discipline techniques used by most teachers will have some degree of success in moderating the behavior of most ADD children, but there will usually be considerable difficulties left. Of course, different teachers will have behavior management systems that work better or worse with particular children.

The degree of difficulty a teacher has with a specific child will be related to the student composition of the rest of the class as well. If the teacher is unfortunate enough to have more than one child with serious behavioral problems, or just a generally "rowdy" or difficult class, his problems with an ADD child will likely be greater. In older grades where the school is departmentalized, the degree of difficulty with a child may depend on the subject taught. Most children behave better in a subject they like, and the degree of stucture (physical education as opposed to math) may be important to the behavior of an ADD child, too.

parental criticism of the teacher

Parents may believe that any teacher, as a trained professional, should be able to handle efficiently the behavior of any child. They may believe that their child should be able to achieve academically, because they sense — usually quite accurately — that the child has sufficient native ability. They don't realize the extent to which impulsivity, distractibility and inattention interfere with the success of the best behavior management techniques, and with achievement. They may directly or subtly convey this disatisfaction to the teacher, and, perhaps, to the administration which can bring further criticism to the teacher.

Because of the tendency of ADD to run in families, some of the parents a teacher deals with may have ADD themselves. ADD adults often have low self-esteem and poor social skills and may show a blaming aggressive attitude, thus making them very difficult people with whom to deal and adding to the total stress of the situation.

the result of teacher viewpoint and frustration

To sum up, the teacher sees a child who is misbehaving deliberately, requiring her to deal regularly with disruptions and to monitor him closely — often resulting in undesirable class climate. His behavior interferes with class progress and the smooth running of the classroom and may bring her criticism. Her self-image as a good teacher may be affected and she may have concern for the welfare of other students and for the future of the ADD child. Though some of the techniques she uses may alleviate some of the difficulties, she is still left with a significant problem for which she sees no solution.

Since the prevailing theory in education, as in the social sciences, has been that undesirable behavior is the result of undesirable experiences, teachers feel encouraged to believe the child's problems are the result of poor parenting or undue stresses in the home. This will be more so in cases where there are signs of problems at home. The teacher can do little to change the situation in the home, but by attaching blame to the home she often lessens her sense of frustration in not being able to rectify the problem. She may also blame the child if she sees his behavior as willful.

The Parents' Point of View

If the ADD child shows his difficult temperament as a baby, the parents' overwhelming feeling during this stage will be exhaustion — the yearning for a good night's sleep and a few hours to themselves. As the child grows and problems develop in the community and school, this creates more difficulty for the parents. In the home, there will be serious problems for the whole family as a result of the ADD child's difficulties.

blaming the child

Although parents are in a better position to see the child's difficulty in paying attention and controlling his impulses, they too will have seen instances when he has controlled himself. He may be stubborn and his misbehavior may seem flagrant at times. Like others, parents may conclude that — at least partly— the child is misbehaving on purpose and could stop if he so made up his mind.

guilt and self-blame about parenting and family stress

The most common response of parents to the problems the child presents is that they must have done something wrong. Most parents are aware of the common feeling in our society that problem behaviors in children are the result of poor parenting or other influences in the home. Although they may have read parenting books or taken courses, they will still remain perplexed by what they are doing wrong. They may feel either that they don't have sufficient patience with the child or that they have spoiled him. The result is that they feel guilty, but don't know what to do about it.

Under the pressure of frustration, one parent may blame the other for either being too lenient or too hard on the child, intimating that this is the source of many of the problems they have with him. It is often the case that the father denounces the mother for spoiling the child. He notices that the boy often behaves better for him. The fact that a child sometimes listens better to his father may be because the child is less familiar with his father (remember, these children often behave better in less familiar situations) and because, in some cases, the punishment dealt out is more severe. (Severe punishment may, however, have undesirable side effects, particularly if used regularly.)

In any case, parents in their frustration may blame each other and will likely feel like failures as parents. This may be particularly hard for a mother whose identity and self-esteem is closely tied to parenting. The guilt parents feel may be accentuated if there has been a divorce or other family crisis which they see has worsened the child's problems.

The self-blame parents feel will usually be amply reinforced in their daily lives by a variety of sources. The responses of aquaintances to the ADD child, whether neighbors, friends, relatives or salespeople, affect the parents as well as the child. When parents ask for understanding or support they may get blame instead. Though often thinly veiled as advice, the blame shows through. Much of the advice will be about consistency and stronger punishment. Some will be about finding alternate ways for the child to express himself, and some of it will be about the fact that he's just "all boy" and parents are overreacting to his normal development.

When the child is young, if he becomes unwelcome in the homes of friends and/or neighbors, this may result in a degree of social isolation for the mother. The mother as well as the child may be ostracized, or she may be unable to get away without the child. She may also feel anger or distance from those who blame her because of the hostility and lack of respect she senses in the blame. Even when blame is couched as advice, it has a way of showing through. As well as having lost an important support system, the mother may be deeply hurt.

Those in the mental health professions are, perhaps, most aware of the ample research and literature establishing the home as a possible source of behavior problems in children. If they feel this to be the case with an ADD child, their attitude and advice may come across as blame. Regrettably, parents often feel blamed by the school as well. Because of the interdependent roles of home and school in the development of the child, this can be particularly unfortunate. Add to this the many books and magazine articles that point the finger at parents as the source of problems with their children, and one can see that parental self-blame and guilt is abundantly reinforced. In talking to parents about their attempts to find help for their child, I have found that the blame and criticism they have received comes up over and over.

other sources of parental guilt
If a parent was hyperactive himself as a child, he may feel badly for having passed on the problem to his child. He may remember an unhappy childhood and fear his child will have unhappy memories as well.

Parents may also feel guilt because at times they dislike and feel angry toward this child who causes them so much trouble. Most parents feel angry toward their children at times, but the anger of ADD children's parents is likely to be more pervasive and is doubly hard to deal with because they feel they have caused the child's problems in the first place.

concern for the welfare of the child
By the time a child has progressed very far in school, parents may have some realistic fears about how he will fare in life. They will have noticed that he is different from other children and more difficult to deal with. They will have seen problems at home, in the community, with peers, and at school and may be beginning to fear permanent psychological maladjustment.

They may start to realize that fulfillment of their hopes for him will be difficult. If he begins to fail academically, they will wonder about his chances for a career. Having noted continuing social problems, they may fear he will always be a social outcast. As he approaches adolescence, they will worry about delinquency and problems with the law. As he gains more responsibilty and begins driving, they may fear he will do something rash that will cause him or others serious injury.

identification with the child

All parents are distressed when they must watch their child in pain — whether it be physical or psychological. In many cases, a certain amount of psychological pain is part of life and is seen to aid in growth. Regrettably, the ADD child will have had more than his share of suffering, and will likely not have learned or grown from it. Rather, it will have lowered his self-esteem and affected his outlook on life. Much of this pain will have been felt by his parents as well.

They will have suffered their child's anguish as he is rejected and ostracized by peers, and his frustration at being unable to do anything about it. His grief and feeling that everyone is unfair and against him when he is in trouble with authority figures will have been perceived as well. As he fails academically, his pain and rage at being called "dummy" may both worry and grieve parents. Such parents will have known the heartbreak of comforting a child who is sobbing, "Nobody likes me," or, "I'm dumb," at the same time knowing the element of truth of these statements. This is all the more disturbing because these chilren are often extremely sensitive to criticism.

parental stress and burn-out

As well as sharing the child's distress, parents find dealing with the ADD child at home exhausting both physically and emotionally. When the child is younger, the constant vigilance and restraint of the child is tiring, as are his tantrums and disobedience. As the child grows older, the conflict continues, only taking on a broader field as parents must deal with problems in the community and school along with much blame directed at themselves.

Problems may develop in the family relating to the stress of having an ADD child. There may be extreme sibling rivalry as other children complain that more is expected of them and they receive less attention. Marriage conflict or breakdown is possible as everyone feels pushed to the end of their rope. Parents may now be at risk of physically or emotionally harming the child. Parenting an ADD child may be particlarly stressful for parents who are ADD themselves and have little patience, a low frustration tolerance and low self-esteem. Such parents may have extreme difficulty in dealing with the child, the community and the school.

result of the parents' point of view

All in all, the parents see a child who is causing them extreme problems and they see no end to this. They may wonder about the amount of control the child has over his actions, noting his seeming control at times. They will often feel criticized and blamed by everyone around them and may not see any way of solving the problem.

In the face of the blame they receive, and the corresponding expectation that they should do something about the child's behavior, some parents in desperation deny that there is a problem. As well, some parents, particularly those who have had similar problems as a child, may minimize or deny the problem because they do not want to admit, even to themselves, the difficult time they had and which their child may have in store.

If parents acknowledge there is a problem, they may try to direct blame away from themselves. Thus, they may blame the child for the problems at home and the school system for the problems at school. They may complain, either between themselves or to the teacher, that the school is expecting too much of the child or that the discipline is not strict enough. Particularly if there has been a divorce, they may continue to blame the other parent as well. Inside, they still blame themselves.

Common Feelings of Child, Parents, and Teachers

The child, teachers and parents all feel excessively stressed by the ADD problem. They all feel frustrated in their attempts to deal with the problem and see no way they can solve it.

From the various points of view, we can see that each sees the solution to the problem as beyond his or her control. The child feels he can't control the negative reactions he gets from his parents and teachers that are causing him pain. Teachers feel they can't control the child's feelings or problems in the home which may be the root of his problems in school. Parent's feel they can't control the child's behavior or the teachers' expectations and discipline. They all feel justified in blaming the others for at least part of the problem. Often they all express blame, subtly or openly, to each other.

the dynamics of blame

Unfortunately, blaming has destructive effects on both the blamer and the blamed. Albert Ellis, Ph.D., and Robert A. Harper, Ph. D., in their book, *A New Guide to Rational Living*, discuss some of the negative effects of blame on all concerned. They explain that whether it is self-blame or blaming others, blame often serves to stop us from looking for solutions to a problem. We may thus miss some steps we could take to alleviate the problem and may not be alert to new possible solutions.

Blaming someone else seems to make it easier to live with a problem we can't solve, but blaming in itself can be a further source of stress. Blaming contains hostility and a lack of respect for the blamed person because he or she isn't behaving as we feel he or she should. However, when we blame someone for a problem — even if that person is in the wrong — it isn't likely to elicit change. In fact, it makes the chance of change more unlikely and encourages retaliation in the form of blame directed back at us or other negative reactions.

Thus, when we express our blame and anger, we will likely have to deal with returned hostility. However, when we bottle up anger, it can have destructive effects on our body. Thus, explain Ellis and Harper, although blame is our natural reaction to some problems, it is a totally irrational response because it doesn't help solve the problem and has an unhealthy effect on all involved (Ellis and Harper 1975, 116).

In the situation of the ADD child, the real loser is the ADD child himself. Everyone blames him and feels his motives are defective. Even though he wants approval and affection like other children (often more desperately so), he often feels blocked in his ability to get it. His self-esteem spirals downward, and he may give up. As well, it is not likely that helpful solutions to his problems will be found while the important people in his life are blaming him and each other, and expecting solutions to come from somewhere else.

Conclusion

The best gift that parents and teachers can present to an ADD child is a non-blaming attitude. This is not to say that because he has little control over his behavior, you let him do anything he wants, but that your attitude says not, "I'll make you behave, because I know you can control your behavior," but rather, "I'll help you behave, because I know it's hard for you."

Then, parents and teachers who want to help the ADD child will continue looking for answers. Much of the present knowledge about treatments and interventions for ADD can be found in the next three chapters. More research is now underway and, hopefully, better answers will be found in the future.

A non-blaming attitude between parents and teachers can increase each one's effectiveness in dealing with ADD problems. Both will benefit from the support and understanding of the other. Respect for each other and an open attitude allows for full communication about details of the problem. It also allows for full cooperation in planning and implementing useful interventions and treatments. As well, it will discourage the child in playing one side against the other as these children sometimes try to do.

Jim Bannard, a psychologist whom I respect very much, works at the Children's Hospital in Calgary, Alberta, where he has helped many ADD children and their parents. He once told me that he always assumes that everyone "does the best they can with the understanding and skills they've got." This, to me, is the essence of a non-blaming attitude. I believe it important to accept others as doing their best even though their values may be different from mine and their skills seem deficient to me.

6

Medical and Other Treatment Options:

Which are the Most Successful?

As Marla approached school age, her mother, a former grade one teacher, worried she wouldn't sit still for five minutes, let alone a whole school period. She was a restless, spirited child who couldn't seem to sit and complete anything and had difficulty following family rules. Knowledgeable in behavior management techniques, Marla's mother had already tried a variety of rewards for good behavior — from praise and attention to happy faces, special trips and coveted toys. None had the desired effect. When Marla misbehaved (which was often), her mother had been doggedly consistent in taking her to her room and depriving her of toys and privileges. She had scolded her and spanked her. Nothing worked for very long.

Marla also had difficulty at playschool in settling down and in getting on with the other children, and her mother recognized in her a pattern of behavior seen in children who did poorly in grade school. Concerned, she began to search for answers. In books on hyperactivity she found descriptions that fit Marla perfectly and symptom lists on which Marla scored high.

Aware that drugs were often used to treat "hyper" children, Marla's parents believed them to be an extreme, last choice alternative — to be used only in very severe cases. They were hoping to find a more "natural" solution.

They got Dr. Ben Feingold's book, *Why Your Child Is Hyperactive* (1975), and the whole family began the prescribed, additive-free diet. Three weeks later, they were delighted to see a mellowing of their daughter's extreme behaviors. She was still, by no means, an easy child, but the diet seemed to calm her and reduce her constant demands and her frequent pestering and aggression toward her baby brother. It relaxed her seeming need to have "exactly what she wanted, right now."

The diet continued to help for another year, but as Marla began to go beyond the home to kindergarden and to friends' houses, her mother found she couldn't control Marla's diet completely, and it seemed that a small amount of coloring or flavoring was enough to set her off for two or three days. Arguments increased at home and there were more problems at kindergarden.

In the meantime, Marla's mother found some current books on behavior management of hyperactive children. They preached firmness and consistency, and suggested techniques similar to those already tried. Disturbingly, some of them suggested that if behavior management techniques were properly used, all would be well. Increasingly aware that all was not well with Marla, and feeling the strain of incessant demands and conflict — along with growing self-doubt — Marla's mother asked her family doctor for a referral to a psychologist who might help her correct what she was doing wrong. The family doctor made the requested referral, but also persuaded her to set up an appointment for Marla with a pediatrician who specialized in hyperactivity.

Much prevailing psychological theory suggested that faulty parenting often caused difficulties such as Marla's and that training parents in parenting skills was the solution. Luckily, Marla's mother encountered a psychologist whose experiences with children like Marla and their parents had convinced him this was seldom the case. He assured her that her parenting was not the problem. He worked with her and Marla's father to restore their self-confidence and find ways to lower the stress they were experiencing. He helped them support each other and keep matters in perspective.

Later, they reviewed family rules and alternate behavior management strategies, and focused on being content in doing their best, though they might have "a tough road to hoe." He made them aware of the possibility of child abuse if they became determined that Marla should behave as they wished. He told them that, in his experience, children who didn't respond initially to behavior management techniques, often did so if placed on medication.

Meanwhile, the appointment with the specialist arrived. He diagnosed Marla as ADD, and explained to her parents how stimulant medication might help her. Her parents decided to try Marla on the medication for a six week trial. Almost immediately her behavior improved. Discipline was still difficult, but conflicts with her little brother and playmates diminished and her parents' firmness had some effect. This gave everyone a breather and family life improved for a while. Her kindergarden teacher also noticed an improvement in Marla's completion of tasks and relationships with the other children.

The year Marla entered grade school, her family moved and they changed doctors. As Marla got older the new doctor advised that she should require less medication and lowered her dosage. At the end of grade three, the doctor suggested she drop the medication altogether as, he advised, she should soon outgrow the need for it. Her parents reluctantly agreed and continued to follow his advice though Marla became increasingly restless, noisy, and argumentative and used much of her excess energy teasing her younger brother. Her loud, rude behavior humiliated her parents in public and embarassed her little brother (by now at school) on the school playground. Marla's grades gradually dropped throughout elementary school, and battles over doing homework increased, but her parents felt hesitant in questioning the doctor's advice.

Without medication and nearing puberty, Marla became progressively difficult to manage and her parents became more distressed. Desperate, her mother tried restricting sugar as she had read this might help. However, she encountered the same problem she'd had with colorings and flavorings: she was unable to control what Marla ate outside the home. She saw no change in behavior.

Her mother had also read about the possible influence of allergies on child behavior and, since Marla was allergic to some medicines, she wondered if she might be allergic to some foods as well. She tried restricting some common food allergens such as milk and grains but found no success in this. She then tried treating her with an expensive herbal oil that was claimed to have diminished hyperactive symptoms in children. As recommended, she tried both rubbing it on Marla's skin and spoon feeding it to her. Neither were successful.

As well, she had read a book by a doctor recommending use of a broad spectrum of vitamins with mega-doses of specific vitamins in which hyperactive children might be deficient. This was not successful either. She even tried allowing Marla to drink coffee as some had said this would help, but it didn't help Marla.

She continued trying various behavior management techniques such as chairing, giving choices, and timing. Some had limited success for a while. Meanwhile, a vicious cycle of escalating coercion (explained in the next chapter) was developing between Marla and her parents and there were continual fights.

Just before Marla began junior high school, the family moved again. She entered a junior high of about 800 students. Here, no one was keeping track of her, and she started to fall between the cracks. She failed to hand in assignments, her marks plummetted, and she began to get failing grades in some of her subjects. Her mouthiness got her into fights. Teachers started to complain that she was disinterested and, though most liked her, some found her disrespectful. The school counsellor was called in.

He tested Marla, found her bright, but thought she had emotional problems that were causing poor performance. He suggested Marla and her parents attend a parent-teen counselling group. Willing to try anything which might help, her parents went to ten weekly sessions where, with group leaders, parents discussed the characteristics and needs of teenagers, as well discipline methods helpful in parenting teens. All of those suggested had already been tried with Marla.

At the same time, Marla attended teen sessions where teens discussed feelings and problems. Some joint parent-teen sessions were held. Some short term improvement in Marla's attitude and marks was noted. The counsellor had suggested, too, that her junior high teachers monitor her school work more closely, and this helped somewhat too.

Next, Marla's mother heard about a company offering help for students with reading and writing problems. Knowing that Marla had both, her mother consulted with these experts and began working with Marla on handwriting, eye exercises and reading skill materials provided by the company.

There was a quick, definite, improvement in Marla's handwriting noted by both her parents and teachers. Her reading improved somewhat, but she refused to cooperate in doing the activities as she found them boring. After three months, her mother discontinued the program, feeling the family was losing more from the constant conflict over doing the activities than Marla was gaining in reading progress.

The reading experts had also noted Marla's squirming and discomfort in sitting still and suggested she may be "tactile defensive." This is a condition where stimulation from clothes or any other impact on the body is unpleasant, or even painful, and is said to cause hyperactive type symptoms. But here again, resistance from Marla made it prohibitively difficult to carry out the suggested therapy and test it.

Feeling growing distress with the level of family conflict and worried about Marla's school difficulties, her mother took her to a new doctor. This doctor agreed that Marla's problems were substantial and suggested medication might help as it had before. Once again, she began drug treatment and an immediate improvement in marks and behavior at school was noted. However, the particular medication used was effective only during the school day and in the evening when the medication wore off, Marla (in what seemed to be a rebound effect) became extremely restless, sassy and argumentative.

The doctor suggested a different medication that would be effectual for more of the day. On this, Marla calmed somewhat and became more receptive to discipline: her parents were then able to implement a new behavior modification program. At present, the medication and behavior program are working reasonably well.

Marla's parents realize that all problems haven't been solved, but they are pleased with the improvements. They have their fingers crossed that one day soon Marla might outgrow her difficulties, but in the meantime, they watch for new developments and new information on ADD.

Marla's story illustrates some of the range of treatment options that have been used with ADD children. This chapter sets out a brief rationale for the use of various treatments from the medical, psychological, and other realms, then explains in more detail, drug treatment and a variety of other less substantiated physiological treatments. The next chapter deals with behavioral management programs that can be used at home and at school to help these children. Chapter Eight explains additional psychological and behavioral interventions that have been found to be useful for some ADD children and their families, and adds some specific educational approaches that can be helpful.

Various Treatments

Although drug treatment has been found to be more effective for far more children than any of the other options mentioned in this chapter (Wender 1987, 55), this is not to suggest that it is, necessarily, the option to be tried first. More "natural" methods are obviously preferable if they can be implemented effectively, and if they work to the extent that the child is having success in the various facets of his life. However, there is danger that using treatments without expert advice may be harmful to a child. As well, experimenting with a variety of treatments (and behavioral interventions) may delay a child receiving more effective medical treatment (Ingersoll 1988, 66). The child will continue to experience conflict, frustration and failure, the effects of which may be difficult to overcome by the time it is realized that medical treatment is necessary.

In Marla's case, her parents feel that much distress and the severity of some problems might have been prevented had she not been taken off the medication. While they believe that other methods were at least worth a try, they regret waiting four years until the situation was critical before they investigated medication again. Although they still have some reservations about medication, they believe it to be preferable to the alternative. They have realized too, that in deciding on treatment for Marla, they must consider the welfare of her little brother, as well, who has suffered much aggression and harassment at Marla's hands.

Often, as in the case of Marla, school personnel or mental health workers will see a child's symptoms to be mainly psychological and refer the child and/or the family for counselling. It is true that most ADD children, particularly those who have not received adequate treatment, will have psychological problems by the time they reach junior high, and many of them will benefit from counselling. Still, in most cases, considerable temperamental problems will remain. As long as the temperamental problems remain, psychological problems will continue to pop up (Wender 1987, 54). Thus, while counselling may be useful to the ADD child and his family, its limitations should be realized, and it should not delay the use of other treatments.

The same holds true for behavior management programs. A behavior management program is usually a useful or necessary adjunct to other treatments, and counsellors, psychologists and social workers can be very helpful in setting up such programs.

For some ADD children (especially those with milder symptoms), a strong behavior management program may be all that is needed. For many, however, this will not suffice. Beware, then, if it is suggested that proper management techniques will be all that is needed or that these techniques, if properly used, always work. Unfortunately, it is sometimes suggested that if psychological methods aren't working, the family is at fault. This can cause much grief and unnecessary guilt and can make the situation considerably worse.

Parents' Reservations about Drug Treatment

Most parents have reservations when they initially consider drug treatment for their child. They find it hard to believe that their child's behavior problem has a physical rather than a psychological basis. Not only does this go against popular notions about the origin of behavior, but it makes the behavior seem less changeable. They forget that some physical ailments respond immediately to drugs, while some psychological scars are not erased by years of psychotherapy.

Parents may also feel that drugs are artificial and unnatural. They may believe that drugs will mask the problem rather than deal with the root of it. They may have heard it suggested that drugs are a "quick fix" or the easy way out of a problem.

Here, it is useful to again note expert opinion as to the likely cause of ADD. If the brain is functioning improperly due to an under-supply of certain brain chemicals, then supplying chemicals which will allow it to function normally is getting at the root of the problem. It is not a "quick-fix"; it is an "appropriate fix."

Furthermore, medication, monitored properly, does not turn a child into an automaton by any means. In fact, the opposite is more the case. ADD can cause a child to resemble a robot set at high speed, careening through life with much purposeless activity, never staying still long enough to finish anything or relate meaningfully to others. When this robot meets an obstacle, it erupts or lashes out automatically, and continues on its high speed, unfocused wandering. Medicine seems to allow children, to varying extents, to relax; to pause, focus, and consider; to become more purposeful in their activity; and to act in ways that accomplish their goals and get them the approval they so desperately need. For parents and teachers there are often still considerable child management problems, but now they have a chance of influencing the child, and the child has a chance of benefitting from the discipline provided.

Parents may also be concerned that their child will become physically dependant on the drug. Dr. Paul Wender, mentioned earlier, a physician who has considerable experience in treating children and adults with ADD, assures us that children never become physically dependent on drugs used to treat ADD (Wender 1987, 57). He explains that a child may be happy with the change the drug has allowed in his life, but that children never like taking this type of medication. They don't get kicks out of it, and they don't get high, instead, they become calmer and more focused (Wender 1987, 60).

Indeed, experts believe that improvements in a child's behavior and self-esteem due to drug treatment will make it less likely he will get involved in abuse of alcohol or other addictive drugs (Moghadam 1988, 53). In addition, when ADD children are treated with stimulant drugs, they tend to steal less in elementary school; display better interpersonal skills and less aggressive behavior; have fewer car accidents as teenagers; and, overall, have feelings of higher self-worth (Ingersoll 1988, 71).

Another type of dependency parents sometimes worry about is the continuing need for medication in order for the child to handle problems and control his behavior. It is true that the medication does not cure the child's problems and he will continue to need medication to help him regulate his behavior as long as his ADD persists. In this way, the child is much like a diabetic who continues to require insulin in order for his body to function properly. While the ADD child's problems are not generally life threatening, they can certainly have serious life consequences. This type of dependency on medication in order to function appropriately is, I believe, preferable to the disablility and its results.

Types Of Drugs Used

There are several types of medicines that may benefit a child with ADD. According to experts, it is impossible to predict how a given child will respond to a particular medication (Wender 1987, 58) so more than one medication may have to be tried. Some medications don't become effective immediately, but seem to require a build-up in the body, perhaps for several weeks, before their benefit becomes evident. Also, behavior will sometimes deteriorate for a while before it improves (Wender 1987, 58). All medications will require monitoring by a physician, who may gradually increase the dosage until an optimal level is reached (Wender 1987, 64).

Stimulant Medication

According to Dr. Wender, the most commonly used drugs in the treatment of ADD are the stimulant drugs. Of these, the most commonly used are *d-amphetamine* (one trade name for this is Dexedrine) and *methylphenidate* (trade name Ritalin). Both are available in short acting and sustained release forms. A less commonly used stimulant drug is *pemoline* (trade name Cylert), which had been used for a number of years in Europe before its introduction into the United States and Canada. Approximately two-thirds of ADD children respond positively to one of these drugs (Wender 1987, 60).

benefits of stimulant drugs

When stimulant drugs work, the ADD child generally becomes calmer, with less purposeless activity, though on the play ground or in other free play situations he is likely to be just as boisterous. However, when restraint and sitting quietly is required he is more able to please. His attention span increases and he is less likely to miss instruction and directions. In school, he is more organized and his work is tidier and more often complete.

Less stubborn and considerably easier to discipline, he can now benefit from positive behavior management, will be less hot headed, and have fewer temper tantrums. Now in times of frustration and conflict he won't carry things so far. If reminded of consequences for a behavior, he will be able to respond appropriately some of the time. He will have some control over his behavior and be able to calm down in situations where, formerly, he responded with escalating anger.

Overall, the effect of the medication is so pervasive that a child may appear to have matured or grown psychologically while the medicine is active. Regardless of this, he will still be the same child with the same personality, habits and interests.

One mother described as "dramatic" the changes seen in her fifteen-year-old son who had been on Cylert (*pemoline*) for six months. Rather than it controlling his behavior, she saw the Cylert as setting him free, as allowing him to decide and control how he wanted to behave.

At school, his marks had improved considerably. He was spending more time with friends, and more friends were coming around. At home, he seemed much happier, and when he disagreed with his parents, his anger and stubbornness didn't escalate until little issues became major blow-ups. His anger no longer consumed him, and he seemed able to see beyond the immediate moment and stop before he brought disagreeable consequences on himself.

To add to this, an educational assessment done with him showed a significant increase in his self-esteem. On a measure of self-esteem, his score had gone from considerably below average the year previous to an average self-esteem score when compared with other fifteen-year-olds. This appeared to be due to his improved sense of control and improved functioning in many areas. Understandably, his parents were delighted.

Unfortunately, problems such as inattentivness or learning problems may persist after medication and require additional interventions, perhaps directed behavior modification or remedial help. Although fights and arguments with friends will usually decrease, positive interactions do not always increase. Here a child may require some work on social skills and in actively building relationships.

side effects

There are some possible side effects to the use of stimulant medication that your doctor will likely tell you about and monitor. For some children, there may be a decrease in appetite and a related degree of weight loss. According to Dr. Wender, normal appetite generally returns after some time, and weight loss never occurs to a medically serious degree (Wender 1987, 67). In most cases, a child's appetite will be normal at breakfast before the drug has taken affect and again at night when the medication has worn off. Because of this, a child should be allowed to eat as much as he wants in the evening.

There have been reports that stimulant medication also decreases the rate of height gain in ADD children. Dr. Wender points out that doctors who have treated ADD children with stimulants from childhood through adolescence have not observed any long term affect of the medication on height. He suggests that if the rate of growth appears to be slowing, the doctor can control this by lowering the dose of medication or advising summer holidays free from the medicine (Wender 1987, 68).

A child on stimulant medication may have trouble sleeping, particularly if a long acting form of medication is used or medication is given late in the day. For this the doctor may want to adjust the timing of the medicine or change the form or dosage.

Dr. Wender states that allergies to amphetamines and *methylphenidate* are very rare, but that one to two percent of children taking *pemoline* will have an adverse reaction to it. This particular reaction can be detected in its early stages only by blood tests, so he recommends children who are taking *pemoline* (Cylert) have blood tests every few months (Wender 1987, 67).

Some parents whose children are on medication say their child has lost some "spark" or "vitality." This is something I have observed as well. I believe the gain in pleasant interactions for the child and family, as well as many other benefits of improved functioning for the child are worth it. Still, this is something that should be discussed with your doctor, particularly if the child appears sad or weepy or becomes noticeably withdrawn.

Other Medications

There are some other types of drugs used for specific ADD children, often because they have other problems besides an attention deficit. These medications include major tranquilizers and cyclic antidepressants, both of which are absolutely non-addictive according to Dr. Wender (Wender 1987, 69 - 72).

Explaining Medication

A child at any age deserves an explanation of why he is required to take medication. However, in explaining the need for medication to treat ADD, one must be careful what one says and implies. We can see that for some children, attending, focusing and organizing themselves can be very difficult without medication. Similarly, no child wants to alienate both adults and peers with offensive behavior and receive frequent punishment, yet these children regularly do just this. Thus, without medication, their impulsivity and need to dominate seem beyond their self-control, even in their own interests. Yet, though the medication can be a great aid, it must not take responsibility for behavior away from the child. The child must know that, though the medication may help, it does not control.

The child's retention of free will should be stressed and explained to him for two reasons. First, a child, particularly as he grows older, does not want to take medication that he feels will control him. He may feel that you are trying to turn him into a zombie that will do exactly what you want him to do. It must be made clear that he can still behave as he wishes; he may still be just as bad as he wishes, as long as he is aware of the consequences. Related to this, it is important that a child understand the medication is being given for his sake, not so others can stand to have him around, (although it would be nice for everyone if he were quieter and more agreeable).

Secondly, it's not a good idea to have a child attribute his actions to powers beyond his control. Here again, it's important to point out that the medication will be helping, not controlling. Have your child think about and list some situations that he would like to change. For instance, would he like to get into less trouble at home? Would he like to be able to pay better attention and do a better job of his school work? As he thinks about these situations, it can be explained he will still be in the driver's seat; it will just be easier now for him to steer the car where he wants it to go.

It should be noted here, that, just as ADD children are usually oblivious to the effect of their behavior on others, they typically will be unaware of their own improved functioning on the medication. Inasmuch as they are usually unreflective on their own conduct, you may have to point out changes to them.

In this regard, it's also important that parents and teachers not explain a child's behavior on the basis of whether or not he's taken his medication. When he's doing a poor job of something or misbehaving they should not say, "Did you have your medicine today?" or, "When did you take your pill?" This implies it is the medicine that is creating his good or bad behavior rather than himself.

Dietary Management

Two-year-old Steven was a holy terror at playschool. He travelled from centre to centre, grabbing toys which he then threw down. He pushed others, pinched and hit. His aggressiveness and activity level suggested ADD, yet there was another explanation for his behavior. He had a new, six-week-old baby sister. In addition to this, his father had deserted the family just before the baby was born, and his mother was distraught. According to her,

Steven's behavior had deteriorated markedly around the time his sister was born and, on top of her other problems, she did not need a "terrible two" gone wild.

The nursery school teacher set up a rigid behavior modification program. She assigned a volunteer mother to keep on Steven's heels. The volunteer stopped him and removed him from the room the minute he began to misbehave. She held onto him and told him why he had been removed. After a few minutes "time-out" she allowed him to return to the room with a clear message as to how he was to behave if he wished to stay. A month of this firm, consistent, behavior management program made not a dent in Steven's behavior. It was true, he didn't cause as many disruptions, because he spent a good deal of time out of the room. However, once returned, he could still be counted on to get into trouble within five minutes.

The fifth week, a changed boy came to nursery school. He was still fairly active, but now he stopped to play quietly at the centres. More importantly, altercations went from their former ten to fifteen an hour to no more than any other child. The teacher was surprised, but pleased, with this sudden reversal of behavior. In discussing with the mother how well the program had modified Steven's behavior, she was startled by the mother's reply. Steven's behavior, his mother said, had changed a few days previous, soon after she removed milk from his diet. He had been allergic to cow's milk as a baby, but around the time his baby sister was born the doctor had recommended he go on milk again as he was over two years old. In her distress, Steven's mother had failed to connect his behavior with the reintroduction of cow's milk. When she mentioned Steven's behavior to her doctor, he had made the connection. In this case, withdrawing a food to which a child was allergic had a dramatic effect on his behavior. At times, allergies have been suggested as a cause of ADD and there are medical people who promote this view.

Others say that the increased activity, restlessness and irritablilty that sometimes result from an allergy, only superficially resemble the symptoms of ADD and that other ADD symptoms will be missing (Wender 1987, 34). While most agree that controlling the foods an allergic child eats may improve his behavior, they maintain that allergic symptoms are not related to ADD. However, it is possible for ADD children to have food allergies in addition to their ADD, and this will make their overall symptoms worse. (Remember, ADD children tend to be allergic.) Treating the allergies may result in partial improvement in behavior, but ADD symptoms will remain (Wender 1987, 34).

If you suspect allergies as a factor in your child's behavior, look for a doctor willing to investigate the problem, or get alternate, competent, nutritional counselling, such as from the local board of health or a registered dietitian. Without this, it is unlikely you will be able to pinpoint allergies, and you run the risk of poor nutrition for your child.

artificial flavorings and colorings, etc.

Perhaps the best known suggestion that diet affects ADD is that of Dr. Benjamin Feingold. In 1975, in his popular book, *Why Your Child Is Hyperactive*, he claimed many hyperactive children were sensitive to artificial food colorings, artificial flavorings, some preservatives, and naturally occurring salicylates (chemically related to aspirin) found in some fruits and vegetables. When such children ate foods containing these substances their behavior deteriorated. For affected children, he recommended a diet free of these elements, and this became known as the Feingold diet.

Since that time, a number of studies have attempted to determine the effectivness of the Feingold diet. Some studies have suggested that improvements noted in behavior may be the result of giving the child more attention, or of a placebo effect (the expectation of positive results which tends to be self-fufilling). However, some well controlled studies have shown that, for some children, removing the named substances improved their behavior and this did not seem to be a placebo effect or the result of more attention (Moghadam 1988, 91). I, as well, have seen positive results from this diet and have talked to a number of parents who believe this diet has improved their child's behavior.

In Marla's case, her parents were quite aware that expectations could affect their observations. However, they expected results of the diet would come within ten days to two weeks as advised by Dr. Feingold in his book. Getting no results within this time, they gave up on the diet, but decided to finish up the special food they had purchased for this experiment. They were taken unaware when they noticed, after three weeks, that Marla's arguing and tantrums had decreased, and that she seemed less driven. To top this off, Marla, for the first time in her four-year-old life, slept through the night.

Hoping to get even better results from the diet, Marla's mother participated in research on the Feingold diet being done by the dietary department of the local childrens' hospital. Here she was given a more extensive list of forbidden foods as well as a restricted list of toiletries, tissues, and nonprescription drugs, none of which had been eliminated in the original Feingold diet. As well, a few tested items were added to the list of allowed foods. Fully expecting an improvement, she instead saw a deterioration in Marla's behavior which was then traced to the bleach in the flour of a newly allowed white bread. Nevertheless, in both of these instances expectations were in conflict with what was observed.

Besides, when Marla returned after the summer to the same playschool she had attended the year before, the teacher, unaware Marla was on a special diet, was amazed. She told Marla's mother there was "the difference between night and day" in Marla's behavior. Other mothers have similar stories.

Regrettably, there are two main problems with the use of this diet, both of which became evident in Marla's case. The first of these is the restrictiveness of the diet. It is a diet to which one must be firmly dedicated in order to make it work. Furthermore, without competent dietary counselling this diet can easily result in nutritional deficiencies.

As mentioned, besides all foods containing artificial colorings or flavorings, and those containing certain preservatives, a number of popular fruits and their juices are restricted. These include apples, oranges, peaches, strawberries and grapes (raisins as well) and corresponding juices. Also a number of common foods are eliminated because tomatoes and tomato juice, sauces, etc. can't be eaten. This eliminates, or greatly transforms, most pasta dishes as well as much Mexican food and many casseroles. Add these restrictions to foods containing artificial coloring, flavorings and preservatives and this leaves a considerably confined list of allowed foods.

This diet works best if the whole family goes on it, rather than just the ADD child. However, one must be prepared for comments such as that of Marla's brother, who had been told that, since Marla was allergic to certain foods, it wasn't fair that the family should eat them in front of her. When yet another additive laden treat had been disallowed, he fumed, "I wish I didn't have a sister. Then I wouldn't have to be on this dumb diet." While this diet does advantageously cut out many "junk" foods, it can become very difficult when other children are having a forbidden treat and your child can't have one. And there are a lot of forbidden treats.

Related to this is the other difficulty in implementing this diet. When a child is young and home all day you can control everything he eats. This changes as soon as he begins to go places on his own. You may deliver a special snack to playschool or kindergarden, which the teacher will see he eats. Yet it becomes increasingly difficult to control what other children share or trade with him. As part of their temperamental package, many of these children are unlikely to obey a parental prohibition, particularly when they find no ill effects (and likely much pleasure) from cheating on the diet.

As he gets older, a child will also object to appearing "different" from other children. When looking at this issue you need to remember that likely, even on the diet, a child will be having difficulty getting on with his peers, and making him unnecessarily appear "different" will not help matters. Few children with allergies have to restrict their fare this drastically, and most will have felt some ill-effects from breaking their diet and can truthfully tell agemates that they get sick or get a rash. These days the term "being hyper" is used in a derogatory manner among children, so a hyperactive child will not want to use that explanation.

sugar

Doctors and others who suggest a relationship between sugar and hyperactive behavior claim that ingestion of sugar (and white flour) causes the level of blood sugar or glucose to shoot up rapidly, then drop to an abnormally low level thus creating hypoglycemia (Smith 1976, 48). Since glucose in the blood is the main energy supply for the brain, an undersupply of glucose results in undesirable behavior. Still, while most doctors agree that limiting sugar and white flour is a good idea, most don't agree with this explanation or believe there is a causal link between sugar and ADD.

Many parents, nonetheless, believe they have seen an improvement in their child's behavior upon resticting his sugar intake. Many teachers have also noted crabby, uncooperative behavior after Halloween and have thought it may be related to high sugar intake as well as excitement and a late night. Remember that many sugary foods are also high in artificial colorings and flavorings.

Also, some research suggests that good over-all nutrition plays a part in behavior and achievement, and some experts suggest that this may be particularly important for the ADD child (Ingersoll 1988, 59). Since good over-all nutrition includes substituting more nutritious foods for sugar-laden ones, it is not clear what part the sugar plays.

nutritional supplements

Those who propose vitamin or health food programs as an answer to ADD either suggest that ADD children are particularly susceptible to poor nutrition or that these children require greater than average amounts of certain nutrients in order to function normally (Moghadam 1988, 93). Following such advice, Marla's mother first tried suggested vitamin supplements. Then reading that faulty absorption of certain oils important to brain function can affect behavior, she fed Marla the needed oil and rubbed it on her skin. While both of these were unsuccessful, other parents I've known have claimed good results from the use of health food programs.

There are a number of possibilities for such positive results. Some health food diets drastically reduce the amount of sugar and artificial flavorings and colorings being consumed by a child. In other cases, such diets may eliminate a food to which a child is allergic or may raise the general level of nutrition for the child. In all of these cases, medical research has documented improvements in the behavior of some children. It may be, however, that some of the particular elements in various health food programs do affect behavior favorably.

coffee treatment

Inasmuch as coffee is a stimulant it might be of use in treating ADD. Studies have not supported the effectiveness of coffee alone as helpful in treating ADD, but some studies have shown that when coffee is combined with stimulant medication, the combination has more effect than medication alone (Wender 1988, 78). The same results can be obtained by increasing the dosage of medicine, however, and doctors feel this is preferable to using coffee, which has a number of undesirable side effects (Wender 1988, 78).

Tactile Defensive Treatment

Some suggested treatments for children with learning difficulties focus on training the senses to overcome the learning problems. Interventions for these types of learning problems are beyond the scope of this book. However, some experts who train the senses as a way to improve learning, feel that the sense of touch may be involved in hyperactive behavior. They say that "tactile defensive" children don't like being touched. They don't like rough clothing, hard chairs or other strong kinesthetic sensations like hot and cold. Therefore, they regularly squirm and fidget, and are often hostile to those who come near them.

To overcome this hypersensitivity it is recommended that one stroke or rub the child's skin for a few minutes each day, gradually increasing the pressure and roughness. An older child could do this for himself. More about this can be found in Svea J. Gold's book, *When Children Invite Child Abuse: A Search for Answers When Love is Not Enough* (1986). While Marla resisted testing this process, other parents have claimed favorable results with their children.

Other Treatments and Interventions

There have been a number of other interventions and treatments suggested for ADD, from banning fluorescent lights and controlling colors in a room to chiropractic treatment and hypnosis. It must be remembered that, in many cases, those promoting a specific treatment have — as well as a concern for the welfare of the child — a vested interest in their program becoming the treatment of choice. Their reputations and their jobs are at stake. Also, while, most programs have at least some parents who say that a particular strategy has made a difference to their child, it should be kept in mind that we all resist the idea that we have been "taken." We are likely to comment that we have seen some benefit from any program we've put time, energy, and/or money into. Remember, too, when it is one's own child who is suffering, desperation may cloud one's judgement.

We must take a hard look at the costs of various plans in terms of time and money as well as possible dangers to a child's health or well-being. As parents, we must investigate options, seek information (from professionals and otherwise) and make informed decisions in the best interest of our child and our family.

Having tried a number of "natural" alternatives, Marla's mother is uncertain as to their benefits. She knows that because of Marla's opposition, some interventions were not given a fair trial. Cooperation, however, is an issue in implementing programs for a good many ADD children and needs to be taken into account.

Marla's mother also believes it quite possible that her lack of precise knowledge about amounts, timing, and length of time to administer some treatments may have caused the poor results. Some experts in the area of drug treatment are pointing to just such variables as causing false results for older research on drug usage. They say that the use of insufficient amounts of medication for too short a time has resulted in drugs previously being judged as non-beneficial for the long-term outlook of children with ADD. They also allege that tests and methods used to determine whether or not drugs have certain beneficial effects are not always accurate or fair (Pelham 1986, 267). Both of these claims could apply equally well to testing of effects of dietary and other treatments. It seems clear in reading the literature that conclusive research has not been done to establish the relative merits of a variety of treatment possibilities for ADD.

Conclusion

This chapter has dealt with a number of treatments, some well researched and strongly proven, some less so. Some of the less proven treatments seem to work for some children, but the success rate hasn't been established and some are expensive and/or difficult to carry out. In pursuing any treatment, it is important to seek the help of a medical doctor or other competent professional.

If you wish to try less proven treatments, with luck, you will find a doctor who is willing to monitor and give advice for your child and help you look at results realistically, one who will be able to explain benefits and potential harms to your child of the various treatments. If, as in the case of Marla, (and in most cases where treatment is used), you and your doctor finally opt for a trial of stimulant or other medication, your doctor will be aware of the needs and problems of your child and your family.

7

Behavioral Management
Programs at Home and at School:

How Do They Work?

In the case of Marla in the last chapter, several interventions often seen in behavior management programs were used. When she was a preschooler, her mother praised and encouraged her and put up charts where Marla was allowed to place stars or happy faces when she behaved in a desirable way. When these tokens by themselves were ineffective, Marla's mother added rewards for an accumulated number of stars or points. She also used a time-out procedure when Marla misbehaved.

Marla showed minimal improvement on a behavior management program before medication was initiated, and when medication was stopped, her behavior again deteriorated despite the continuation of behavior management. As a teen, Marla was put back on medication, and once again became more amenable to a behavior program for continuing problems. Marla, like a number of children I've known who have shown little improvement on behavioral management programs without the use of medication, showed a strong pattern of escalating aversive behavior.

Escalating Aversive Behavior Patterns
The feature of ADD that parents usually find most difficult to endure is the continual aversive behaviors these children display. Aversive behaviors include crying, screaming and tantrums, whining, arguing, damaging furniture, walls or other items, and hitting, kicking or biting a parent who is trying to deal with them.

Some experts believe these children display such behaviors in order to force or coerce a parent into giving them what they want.

Most children display these behaviors some of the time, but ADD children display them considerably more often and to a greater extreme. ADD children often explode into a tantrum or furious argument when a parent asks them to do a task such as the dishes or to come home from playing. They show similar behavior if they want to go somewhere such as a park and the parent says "no"or when they want an ice cream cone or toy at the store. Perhaps the most frequent instance of oppositional screaming and fighting is when they are being disciplined.

A parent's response to such behavior is often a restatement of the command or denial, this time in a louder, sterner voice. With many children this works. With ADD children it does not. These children then escalate their aversive behaviors. If they were crying, they may begin screaming. The next step for many parents who are trying to be firm with their child is to shout at the child or spank him. For regular children, if the stern voice didn't work, this usually will. For ADD children, it may work part of the time, but sometimes only if the parent becomes incensed or spanks very hard — and sometimes, not then. At this point the parent may lose control as the ADD child continues his aversive behavior.

When parents are angry with them, regular children usually display some sort of de-escalating behavior such as lowering their heads, pouting, or crying. Alternately, they may try to negotiate with the parent, "Can I stay ten more minutes, then I'll come home?" or they may "drag their heels" as they reluctantly cooperate with the parent's wishes. ADD children, however, show a lack of de-escalating behaviors. While the ADD child may try to negotiate, he does it in an aggressive, argumentative style, and if the parent agrees, he will often "up" his request. In fact, at times, it seems that the ADD child wants an argument as much as he wants the item or privilege requested.

I remember watching a five-year-old hyperactive boy whose mother brought home two small windmills, one red and one blue. When the mother announced this, the boy immediately said, "I want red." However, when his three-year-old sister, being very cooperative, said, "I want blue," he immediately changed his request, stating that he wanted blue instead. His sister had enough and stood firm with the blue. Because of the fuss he created, this boy ended up with a spanking and was sent to his room with no windmill.

While regular children often take conciliatory action to appease their parents or perhaps stomp away angrily or do a job begrudgingly, the ADD child seems spurred on to greater heights of anger by his parents' firmness. What often happens is that both parent and child escalate their negative behavior in order to "win." And in many cases, each will win at different times. In other words, some of the time the child will give in and do as he's told, while other times the parent will give up and the child will get out of doing a task he doesn't want to do or will get what he wants. Some experts say that because the child wins some of the time, this encourages him to continue his aversive behavior (Barkley 1985, 180).

This may be so in some cases. However, I have seen more than one child use strongly aversive behavior for more than a year, never having it get him what he wanted, yet continuing just as strongly. And punishment of the aversive behavior made little difference to these children. I have seen children in these circumstances lose control completely. They seem not so much trying to coerce a parent or teacher as venting their frustration in blind anger. In these cases, the behavior seems aversive (oppositional, negative, protesting), but not necessarily coercive (planned to force a change of mind). It seems this blind rage relates to the child's low frustation tolerance, and to his emotional instability.

Add to this the fact that many of these children showed extreme aversive behavior (strong, frequent crying and fussing) as infants before there was much chance for reinforcement to take place. In fact, regular babies likely receive more reinforcement for their crying and fussing because the actions parents take are able to satisfy the babies' needs — so the protests of regular babies get them what they want. In the case of ADD babies, parents are often unable to find a means to comfort them when they fuss, and thus their crying is unsuccessful in bringing them satisfaction. It would seem, ADD babies recieve less reward for their aversive behavior, and yet it continues stronger than in children who were consistently rewarded (comforted) for such behavior.

Although, in some cases at least, reinforcement seems irrelevant to the amount of negative behavior a child displays, the child's negative behavior may influence parents so they are less likely to make the same request of the child again. For instance, if a mother and child are visiting and it is time to pick up toys, the mother is likely to pick them up herself rather than ask it of the ADD child. This is because, the last twenty times she asked him to do this job at home it turned into a major conflict and the child ended up in his room. In order to avoid a scene including having to pick him up and carry him away kicking and screaming with the toys still not put away, she will not ask him to do it. It is possible that the ADD child realizes this connection. This seems unlikely though because of the lack of foresight in general these children show.

At school as well, the frustrated ADD child may erupt into angry, aversive behavior which disrupts the class and can be very difficult for the teacher to deal with while she monitors the rest of the class. These tantrums may not be as severe, however, as those at home partly because peer censure serves as a strong, immediate penalty (the kind that works best with an ADD child) and partly because the situation is less familiar.

The following example further illustrates the considerable difficulty parents encounter in trying to deal with the ADD child's behavior and, at the same time, live a reasonably normal life. Four-year-old Billy's mother has a doctor appointment for him at ten o'clock. Billy is still in his pyjamas, so at a quarter to nine his mother tells him he should get dressed. He immediately argues that he doesn't want to — he is busy playing with his toys. She tells him the reason, takes him by the arm, and firmly repeats her request. At this point, he flies into a tantrum. The mother has been trying to get her six-month-old baby as well as Billy's two-year-old brother ready for the outing, so perhaps has only ten minutes to deal with this problem. She also anticipates time will be taken by further problems when it is time to get into the car.

She has some choices. She can tell him he must go to his room until he gets dressed. This will, she knows, involve dragging him kicking and screaming there and locking him in, and entails a strong possibility that he may not be ready in time, so she will have to forcibly dress him at the last moment.

Another possibility is offering him a reward such as an ice cream cone after the visit at the doctor's. The problem here is that this reinforces his protesting behavior. Even if she made this offer before he protested, it could encourage him to expect something every time he complied with a small request, and it will, she knows, entail him whining for the ice cream all the time they are at the doctor's. It might be reasonable to say she will buy him an ice cream cone if he gets dressed and behaves well at the doctor's, but this is too much good behavior over too long a time for many ADD children to handle. When the time comes for the ice cream cone to be denied, there is likely to be another tantrum, and this one in public.

A further possibility, the one many mothers choose when they need prompt action or when they have lost patience, is that of aversive behavior aimed back at the child with the objective of coercing the child to comply. Of the three choices, this is the one that has the best chance of working quickly without a prolonged fight, and it's carry-over to the next time is as good as for the other choices.

Thus, the mother may yell at Billy, threaten dire consequences, or spank him. Some of the time the first two will coerce him into doing as she wishes, but she will have to keep escalating these as time goes by. Sometimes she will have to spank him until he complies, which may require a very hard spanking or several spankings, as he does a little and then stops, and may take her into the realm of child abuse.

Moreover, this type of coercive behavior on her part encourages further aggressive behavior in an already aggressive child, especially if used often. Furthermore, the escalating aversive behavior of both mother and child will result in a conflict ridden atmosphere much of the time. This is draining for the parent, and will destroy the child's self-esteem as he feels the brunt of such regular hostility.

Thus, it seems, none of these avenues offer an effective, reliable way for a parent to deal with extreme aversive behavior of some ADD children. As mentioned earlier, neither may a behavior management program work very well for a child who goes completely out of control unless the child is first placed on medication. Medication seems to effect the ability of the child to actually think and comprehend during times of conflict and anger. Then, if he knows there is a consequence attendant on misbehavior, he may be able to control himself to avoid it, and if he misbehaves, he usually will cooperate in the consequences. Though he may still misbehave, he will have a chance to learn from the program.

This said, there are a number of behavioral interventions one can make that for some children may suffice to manage their behavior without medication and allow them success in the various areas of their life. As well, children who have responded positively to medication can often benefit greatly from a behavior management program. These are the children who are still very difficult, (but not near-impossible anymore) to handle. For other children with severe symptoms, medication doesn't work, and for those children, a strong behavioral management program may help and should be given a try.

Even in cases where behavioral management techniques have little effect on the child's future behavior (he doesn't seem to learn from it), there can be other advantages. Behavioral systems allow a consistent, moderate approach to the child and his problems. Parents can use such techniques knowing that they are taking an active stance and following the recommendations of experts. Of course, this will require an acceptance of the fact that neither we nor the experts have all the answers — only best choices for now.

An important pay-off for using such a system will be in terms of the child's self-esteem, which will suffer less if a non-demeaning, non-aggressive method of control which respects him as a person is used. Parents consciously using these techniques (with full recognition that there may be little permanent change in the child's behavior) are less likely to succumb to the frustration and futility we all feel when we can't accomplish what we'd like to. They will be more able to keep matters in perspective and withstand the criticism (whether it be subtle or overt) of others.

There will be less anger and frustration expressed toward the child, and the family atmosphere will be healthier for everyone. This is not to say that all but a few saintly parents will not lose their patience and temper on occasion. When this happens parents should try to assess the situation, determine if something could be done to prevent a reoccurrence of the anger, then promptly forgive themselves. If recurring anger and conflict is becoming a pattern, however, counselling for the parents and/or children can be very helpful.

Considerations in Initiating a Behavioral Program

As mentioned, the severity of the child's behavior, especially the escalating aversive behavior, is important in deciding on a behavioral program, as is whether medication has already been tried. Other realistic considerations are the amount of time parents have available and the stamina of the parents, as many behavioral interventions require considerable time, organization and fortitude.

Some may criticize parents who have found they don't have the necessary time or stamina to consistently enforce a behavior management program. Usually, however, these people have never had to deal with the constant rule infractions and aversive behaviors some ADD children display on a daily basis. Some experts who work with parents find it is usually impossible for a single parent to find the time and energy necessary to carry out an effective behavior management program (Moghadam 1988, 62). It may also be very difficult if both parents are working or for other reasons.

It tends to be easier to run behavior management programs at school than at home because a teacher has the child in her sight and under direct control most of the day. However, a large or particularly difficult class may make such a program unmanageable, and teachers vary in organizational skills and stamina just as parents do. Even the hardiest, most organized teacher can find it impossible to constantly monitor a behavior management program while running a class.

Before deciding on a behavior management program, testing should be done to determine the mental abilities of the child and to look for learning disabilities. Some or all of the restless, unfocused behavior, particularly at school, may be due to expectations that are inappropriate. Corrective programming may eliminate the need or change the focus of behavioral programs or other treatments.

When instituting a behavior management program, the aim should be for gradual improvement over many months. Since many children slip back if the program is discontinued, it needs to be recognized that there may be a long-term requirement for some type of program. Because of the ADD child's need for novelty and because the needs of the child change as he matures, it may work best to use a variety of programs over the years.

The Design of Behavior Management Programs

Sometimes called behavior modification programs or token or point systems, behavior management programs consist basically of a set of rules and corresponding rewards (positive consequences) for following the rules and, sometimes, punishments (negative consequences) for not following them. They can be designed by psychologists, teachers, parents or others who are familiar with the principles. Some experts suggest that punishments or negative consequences are not necessary in such systems, because they believe that misbehavior can be extinguished by ignoring it. This may be true for the unwanted behavior of some children, but it is seldom true for the misbehavior of ADD children. Because of the severity of problems, a combination of both rewards and punishments is generally more effective.

Communication between Home and School

Close communication between home and school can be helpful to all concerned. Rules, rewards and punishments can be discussed and information on the child's progress can be shared as parents and teachers provide support for each other. Continuing communication can be facilitated through the use of a day book taken back and forth from home to school by the child. In this, teachers can relate how well the child behaved at school each day and this may or may not be rewarded at home. Parents can send back comments they feel may be helpful to the teacher.

However, when parents are responsible for consequences related to school behavior, the time lag between the behavior and its consequence may make this procedure ineffective. Moreover, it often works better to have the child see himself as primarily responsible to his teachers at school and his parents at home. Notwithstanding this, it helps some children if they receive reinforcement at home for good behavior at school. This might consist of parents' recognition and praise when a child has done well on a day or in a week and ignoring the report if he hasn't.

Reports from teachers on school behavior can be facilitated by developing a check list and running off copies. Such a list can use either yes and no or a rating scale. If homework or being on time for school is the problem, the teacher can check either yes or no. For other behaviors such as quality of class work, and behavior in class and on the playground a rating scale from one to four might be used, with one standing for excellent and four for very poor. For the most part, it is more effective if the teacher can administer a program for school behavior with the day book used to support the program, rather than relying on parents to administer consequences. Most teachers are familiar with behavior management programs and many use them in their classes. A sample home program and a sample school program will be described later.

Rules

Rules for a behavior management program need to be detailed, precise and clear, but at the same time be as few and as simple as possible. They should always be written down and kept in a central place for easy referral. It is also a good idea to make a copy for each child, and to have a spare copy stored in a secret location. (You could also include a penalty if the rules "disappear.") The written copies should include a list of rules, a list of rewards for following the rules and a list of penalties for noncompliance.

It is important that they be spelled out very exactly. An ADD child, with his penchant for arguing will take advantage of any ambiguities. If you assign the child the job of setting the table, you must put down precisely what this means. Does it mean only place settings, or does it include center dishes as well, and if so, which centre dishes? If you have a rule that says "No rude behavior allowed," or phrased more positively, "Be polite to everyone in the family," you may have to list specifically as many prohibited behaviors as you can. Then you will have to state, additionally, that parents are the judges in cases not mentioned.

It is a good idea to start with only one or two rules and work up from there. The easiest ones to enforce are a good idea at the beginning. Take for example a rule stating " __ will do the dishes on Monday, Wednesday and Friday. This includes . . . (list all steps). They are to be started within ten minutes after everyone finishes eating, unless __ has recieved permission otherwise." This rule is easy to clarify and it is easy to determine whether or not it has been followed. However, if there is a great deal of conflict around this issue in your household, start with something else.

The ADD child is likely to have many areas of behavior that could use improvement. It is best to pick ones to work on that are really important to you as a parent or teacher. Because of the difficulties parents have had with an ADD child, they are often more controlling and negative and the ADD child will have received more punishment than other children. This much negative attention will lower the self-esteem of any child and lead to further problems. Although a behavior management program tries to eliminate conflict, things don't always go as smoothly in practice as they sound on paper, and it is best to eliminate as many potential areas of conflict as possible right from the start. Thus you might allow a child to slam doors, but not damage any family possessions. You might not worry about perfect table manners, but be concerned that homework is done.

For expediency, written rules should cover only essential, important behaviors. There are a number of other techniques which are not so time consuming in enforcement which can be used for lesser issues you feel must be addressed and for problems that pop up. Some of these techniques will be discussed in the next chapter.

In deciding on rules you must consider how obvious infractions will be. If you are going to have a rule, "Brush your teeth every morning," then you must have a way of determining if this has been done. If this is an area of difficulty, you may have to stipulate that teeth must be brushed before a specific time, and then inspect at that time every day. Alternately, you could require brushing be done in the kitchen so a parent can know it has been done. You may have to be careful, depending on the age of the child, that he does not see this rule as unfair or unusual.

Rules need to be fair and reasonable in terms of the child's experience. An eleven-year-old knows that other children his age don't have to brush their teeth under the watchful eye of a parent, and may feel this an insult to his maturity. It does need mentioning that many ADD children will claim all rules are unfair and unreasonable when they don't want to follow them. However, they aren't so likely to "dig in their heels" if the rules require behaviors common to others their age. (But you should probably use sources other than their word as to what is expected of peers.)

Rewards or Reinforcers

Many behavior management programs use points or tokens and some method of keeping track of how many a child has earned. A stipulated number of points or tokens can then be exchanged for privileges or items the child would like.

A simple chart can be made where points can be tallied or an abacus or any type of counting device can be used to record points. Ease of use is important. The abacus doesn't require a pencil be found each time it is used. However, it will likely require that the child can't reach it and add points at will. A point system is often used in the home with children over eight, and may be more manageable at school than a token system, though, possibly, not as motivating.

A token system can be more motivating for young children if they are given something they can actually handle and put in a container or on a chart themselves. Tokens can be anything moveable that can both be rewarded and taken away. Peel and press pictures and plastic poker chips make good tokens. Tokens should not consist of items readily available to children. Awarding tokens can be time consuming, and this should be considered, as should any possibility a child could have access to their storage area. This is not so likely at school where students and the storage area are in view of the teacher at most times.

Alternately, a teacher or parent can put tokens awarded in a designated spot within the child's view. A rule specifying when they may be counted might be necessary, as children become eager to earn them. For some children, earning a given number of tokens can be almost as rewarding as the end reward. This is especially true at school where everyone is aware of the number of tokens each child has.

It is important that the points or tokens come to have a reward value in themselves, as it is the token rather than the eventual reward that follows on the heels of a behavior. A good way to encourage a reward value for tokens or points is to give praise and attention, which act as social reinforcers, when awarding points. Another way is to use happy face stamps or stars which have reward value in themselves or, as mentioned earlier, a concrete token.

In many token systems, a child starts with zero tokens and accumulates tokens until he has enough to trade in for a stipulated prize or privilege. Therefore, a child who loses points might run up an IOU before he gains points. A better way of doing this is to start with a given number of points that are free, but can be lost.

It is important that prizes be seen as rewarding by the children, not just by teachers or parents. One way to ensure this is to list examples of possible prizes and privileges and ask the children which they would like. You could also make available a variety of prizes and privileges from which the child can choose.

At home the most appropriate and effective prizes are the normal day to day privileges that children enjoy. These would include such things as watching TV, having a special snack, talking on the telephone, and riding a bike. Small toys, can be offered or more expensive clothes than usual, but one has to be careful not to let prizes escalate in price as this can become very expensive, and artificial — it seems out of proportion to award a bike for a week's good behavior. As well, the more immediately a reward is given, the better it works with these children: ADD children generally need to be able to earn their prize by about a week — for younger children less than that.

If a child wants a special, expensive item such as a bike, skateboard or video game system, parents can buy the item, then let the child rent it on a weekly basis. If the child follows the rules and earns a certain number of points in a week, then he is able to rent that item for the next week. Otherwise it will be locked away or off limits for the week. This can also be done on a daily basis: if rules are followed one day, then the item is available to the child the next and so on. Some ADD children may require daily rewards for them to be immediate enough so the child will work for them. Others are capable of earning points all week for one reward. This plan can work well if you can find an item the child values very much.

A special reward or privilege can also be tied to one rule such as doing chores or homework each day — something that is a major concern or problem. For some children, tying allowance to doing their chores works well, with partial payment for partial work. When possible, it is a good idea to have the reward related to the rule. For example, if a child puts away his bike and other toys or items (showing he cares enough for his possessions to put them away), then he is allowed to ride his bike (one of his possessions) the next day.

At school, privileges can be used as reinforcers too. Depending on what is customary, the child may lose the privilege of being out of his seat if he does not behave while there. Free time is another possible privilege rewarded if all work is done acceptably, and behavior has been acceptable.

So is permission to pick a desirable activity such as a game from a special shelf. Most of these children need their recess as a time to blow off steam, so losing this privilege should be saved for serious behaviors or used only for a limited time. If a child is consistently unable to earn recess privileges, then recesses should be dropped from the list of benefits the child must earn. The same is true of missing school activities that the child enjoys such as films, field trips or physical education. However, if the child behaves badly at recess or during a special activity it makes sense to deprive him of this activity for the duration of the period or for its next period.

Rewards or positive consequences can be likened to adults receiving pay cheques if they do an efficient job at work. Adults earn privileges such as driving a car. To keep their licenses, they must follow driving regulations. Otherwise they must relinquish the privilege of driving, and their licenses are taken away for a period of time. They also lose money or their freedom if they don't act in a responsible, caring manner. Whether these situations involve loss of a privilege or application of a punishment depends on how you look at them. ADD children generally respond better to the idea of a lost privilege.

You may find that using everyday privileges as rewards works very well over a long period of time, especially if you add privileges as the child gets older. However, in some cases, especially if you are using special items or toys as rewards as well, you will have to change the rewards fairly often as interest in them begins to wane. This is especially relevant to rewards in behavior programs at school. ADD children lose interest in toys and motivating activities much faster than other children.

Don't forget the social rewards of attention and praise. These children in particular need positive attention. Whenever they are given a reward or privilege, be sure to team it with lots of praise. While many children will work solely for praise, most ADD children will not. Still, praise is important both at home and at school, and we can forget to give it if we are thinking only about the other rewards these children are working for. When a child is doing school work, a job that takes some time, or has behaved well for some time on a family outing, comment regularly on how well he is doing.

It is more meaningful and sounds more sincere to praise the accomplishment rather than the child. Thus comments like "I noticed you've kept right on working for the last ten minutes. Keep up the good work!" or "I see you've been quiet and polite since we arrived. Good going! Keep it up!" are better than telling the child he is a good boy. Rewards may have to be given initially for small steps toward an eventual goal, so in the beginning, one might reward ten minutes work or the child's ability to get through supper without annoying his sister. As the child improves, expectations can be raised.

Punishment or Response-Cost

As has been explained, many consequences to behavior can be looked at either as punishment, or as loss of a privileges — with the loss of privilege concept working best for most ADD children. Another way of looking at negative consequences, however, is in terms of a fine for bad behavior or a "response cost." If a child behaves or "responds" in a certain way, it will "cost" him something. Generally it will cost him a privilege. For some children, this ties together the behavior and consequence better than other explanations.

There are some consequences that children generally see as punishing. You could refer to a spanking as the loss of a privilege not to have someone hit you, but this doesn't make much sense. Being sent to one's room and being grounded fall into the category that most children see as punishing. They have similarities to being sent to jail as an adult, which is commonly seen as a punishment as opposed to a loss of the privilege of freedom.

When a child is young, there may be occasions when a mild spanking is useful. This is true of behaviors you need him to stop immediately such as running into traffic or kicking the baby. As a general method of applying consequences, however, it would have to be used much too often, and can have effects more undesirable than the original behavior.

It has been found that children whose parents use physical punishment regularly are more likely to use physical aggression as a way of solving problems. Most criminals who assault others have been assaulted themselves as children — often within the family. Many ADD children already show a tendency toward physical aggression; use of physical punishment against them is likely to reinforce this. Moreover, because the behavior of an ADD child can be extremely annoying, there is always the danger of going too far with physical punishment.

Time-out is a good method of handling such things as arguing, fits of temper, and fighting or other aggressive behavior. The time-out can be explained as a cooling off or thinking period rather than as punishment. This may make it easier for the ADD child to accept. It will also set a tone of helping the child improve his behavior, rather than punishing him because he's bad.

Some children don't mind being sent to their rooms, especially if they are stocked with lots of toys. At school, they may enjoy visiting with other children or watching activities if sent out of the room. I remember one boy whose class was in a portable classroom which had a door, opening directly outside. If he misbehaved and the teacher sent him out of the room (done in warm weather only), he would get his bike out of the nearby bike rack and ride around having a great time.

A better plan is to have a "thinking chair" or a "quiet chair" where the child is required to sit out for a length of time and think about how he might improve his behavior. The chair should face the wall and offer a limited view, although the parent or teacher should be able to easily see the child. Not going to the chair immediately should result in the time being lengthened. Moving noticeably, or making noise should result in the timer being reset. It may be necessary to require that they sit on their hands or fold their arms.

When the time on the chair is up, the child should be required to tell the adult why he was there and how he can avoid going back. If he is unwilling to do this, he should stay on the chair until he can do so. If another child in the family or at school interacts with a child on the chair, that child should be required to sit on another chair for a predetermined amount of time. For children under five, five minutes on the chair is usually long enough. For children five to ten, ten minutes should be required and for those over ten, fifteen minutes. Used consistently, this can be a very effective way to handle some behaviors.

A Sample Behavior Management System for Home Use

The behavior management system which will be described was designed for a thirteen-year-old ADD child. Because there was a good deal of sibling rivalry in the family, and because the rules were family rules, his sister, eleven, was included in the plan to make it fair.

Looking at the rules, you will realize that a major issue being tackled in this family is arguing and other aversive behavior. While some rules may appear arbitrary, for some ADD children this is necessary. If there is any room for argument, these children will argue.

Unfortunately, this child was not put on medication until he was thirteen and the family conflict was severe. This child was volatile and persistent and the parents had little success in using behavior management techniques prior to the medicine. The medication gave them new hope that they would be able to influence his behavior, as he now seemed more aware of others and had slowed down enough to listen. He no longer carried every small issue so far that he ended up being punished. According to the parents, with the child on medication, this program worked well, and after about three months they were able to omit the daily recording of behavior, but they still applied consequences as laid out.

They made separate lists of rules, privileges and rewards for following the rules, and penalties for breaking the rules. They made four copies of each: one for each child, a working copy which was kept on the refrigerator, and an extra copy they put away. The program is outlined below.

rules

1. Be polite to everyone in the family. Parents are judges of what is polite. (The family had already discussed a number of behaviors that would be considered rude.)

2. Do your assigned jobs. Clean your room when asked. (The parents felt clean rooms were not a priority, so children were only asked to clean them about every month or so. This and other chores were detailed for each child in another list.)

3. Do the things your parents ask you to *right away* without complaining. (It had been agreed that parents would impose a suitable time limit on each request if necessary.)

4. No arguing with your parents about anything. No asking, "Why?" about what you are told to do or told you can't do. This is considered arguing. (The repeated asking of, "Why?" had turned into aversive behavior, so children were not allowed to ask this, although when relevant, parents still told the children why they were asked to do things and why certain behaviors weren't allowed.)

5. Stay out of your parents' relationship with your brother or sister. No complaining about how the rules for your brother or sister are carried out. (A common response of this ADD child to a request or consequence was that his sister in some way had it easier. The child's arguing was egocentric and illogical, but stubbornly entrenched. Under the guise of demanding fairness he presented more aversive behavior.)

6. Ask before you watch TV or leave the yard. (This rule underlined the fact that watching TV and going out was a privilege that had to be earned.)

7. Ask before you eat any food that is not on the list on the fridge. (This helped make special snacks a privilege.)

8. Clean up after yourself. An area should be left in the same condition in which you found it.

regular privileges

1. Watching TV and leaving the yard are privileges that must be asked for each time. Other privileges that may be lost: playing pool, playing Nintendo, talking on the telephone, having a radio/tape recorder in your room, and having a telephone in your room.

special privileges and rewards

1. Renting a movie.

2. Going to a movie.

3. Pizza or other special supper.

4. Special snacks.

5. Being taken somewhere you want to go.

6. Other special activities that come up.

When granting these rewards and privileges parents will consider behavior during the past day and the past week.

penalties

1. For not cleaning rooms as directed within the time limit set — lose tape recorder and telephone for one day and then until job is done.

2. For not doing other jobs within the time limit set — lose all privileges and must do the job in question plus another assigned job before you get privileges back. If parents must do a job because it needs doing right away, two more jobs are added to your list. *Jobs this refers to are: regular chores, jobs your parents have asked you to do, and cleaning up after yourself.*

3. For arguing or complaining or for being rude to people or destructive of possessions — fifteen minutes on the thinking chair with timer to be reset for movement or noise. If you don't go to the chair immediately when asked — one day grounding and loss of telephone privileges. If arguing persists after grounding, more days may be added. (Parents have to be careful here, not to use up this effective consequence on one issue. Usually a maximum of three days grounding is as effective as more.)

4. For taking a privilege (TV, leaving yard, or special snack) without asking — lose all privileges for one day or more.

To keep track of behavior, this family used a check-list chart made on an ordinary lined paper sheet and kept on the refrigerator. On the lines along the left-hand side of the page they wrote in names of the days for four weeks. Across the top they summarized each desired behavior and made a column for each. Each day, either during the day as behavior occurred, or as a summary at night, parents put a check mark or an x under each behavior. Sometimes there was more than one check or x under a certain behavior on a given day. There was also room for a brief comment if necessary under each behavior. When a request was made for a special privilege such as a movie, the chart could be consulted about behavior that week or month.

The parents in this family found the penalties or loss of privileges more effective and easier to administer, than setting up rewards or special privileges for a predetermined number of points. Therefore, they used their reward system in a more general way than is recommended in most behavior modification programs. However, this system worked well for this busy family. When granting a privilege, parents consulted the chart on the refrigerator and commented on behaviors on which their decision was based, in this way pointing out that privileges were the result of good behavior. If parents or teachers have time to record and keep track of points, you may find this an added benefit. This can be particularly useful if used for one behavior that is a significant problem to the family.

A Sample Token System for School Use

Like many teachers, I have tried a number of reward and response-cost systems with students. I have used them with classes of over thirty students, with individual children pulled out of a regular class, and with groups of eight to ten students. I have found token systems to work to varying degrees for many students with behavior problems, not only those with ADD. The token program which I will outline shortly is one that I have developed using recent guidelines published by experts in the area of ADD, and combining these guidelines with the reality of the school situation and my experience in working with numbers of these children. However, this program is intended as a sample program only and will need adaption for individual students and groups.

In classes of around thirty children — including a few children with behavior problems — I have generally used a point or token system with the whole class. However, a program could be designed for one or more individual students. Two of the issues here are the possible jealousy of other students if special rewards or privileges are used and the increased negative image the "problem" student may gain depending on how the program is presented to the rest of the class.

When using such a system with the whole group it can be prohibitively time consuming to keep track of and award points to individual students (though I have done so). It generally works better to group students into teams. Students with behavior problems can be grouped with relatively well-behaved students. It sometimes works better to have each behavior problem student form a group of one. It can be explained that these students are having particular difficulty and the teacher wants to monitor and help them individually. The students in a class already know which children are behavior problems, and a frank discussion can set a tone of helping these children as opposed to making them behave.

In such a program, it is important to encourage a cooperative atmosphere rather than competition. Thus, I have found it important to reinforce students helping others — including those on other teams — to behave according to the rules. Ignoring the misbehavior of others can be rewarded as can giving "build ups" and encouragement to others or the class in general. It is beneficial to encourage regular students to be helpful and somewhat tolerant toward children with behavior problems, but at the same time, to expect that these children can and will learn to behave more acceptably.

Most of my experience with regular class groups and small groups has been at the primary level (grades one to three). The program I will outline here is an example of a program for a primary level group of eight to ten students with learning and behavior problems. While a teacher designing a program for any student, group or class will want to consider individual and class needs, there will be other issues for higher age groups — including the greater sophistication of older students and increased peer pressure. The damage that criticism and "put-downs" from peers can do to an ADD child should not be underestimated and should be taken into account in setting up any program.

rules

To gain insight into how students perceive various rules as well as student cooperation, I seek student input when deciding on class rules. This doesn't mean that all student suggestions are incorporated into rules or that any rules I believe to be important are missed. Some ideas I accept as good suggestions, though I don't write them down. At other times, I give a suggestion along with a question as to whether anyone can see any problems with the particular rule I see as necessary. When possible, I phrase the rules positively.

I transcribe the rules in large print to be placed in a prominent place, and to be reviewed periodically. I generally put beside each rule a symbolic diagram to illustrate the rule. This isn't only to help students who have limited reading ability, but is more meaningful to visual learners, and is a quick reminder for everyone. It is quicker to glance up and see a picture of stick figures holding hands than it is to read, "Be polite, kind and helpful to others." I find students learn the rules each picture symbolizes very quickly.

The rules students and I formulate "together" are similar to the following:

1. Be polite, kind and helpful to others. Give "build ups." (Diagram of stick figures holding hands and smiling.)
2. Don't argue with teachers. (Diagram of scowling stick figure. Its open mouth has a red x on top of it.)
3. Only one person talks at a time. (Diagram of a group of smiling faces. Only one has its mouth open.)
4. Look at the person who is talking. (Diagram of two wide open eyes.)
5. Listen carefully. (Diagram of two big ears.)
6. If you want talk, put up your hand. (Diagram of stick figure with hand up.)
7. No running or cheving gum in the school. (Diagram of running stick figure and of a packet of gum — each have a red x on them.)
8. Work hard and do your best job. (Diagram of a star.)

Teachers will have their own rules and ways of formulating them. The important issues for the ADD student are that he feels he has had a say in the rules and that he knows exactly what they mean. In my class, we discuss reasons for rules and situations that they cover. In the above list, rules number one and eight are the most open to interpretation. We do some role playing of various behaviors that might be kind or unkind, helpful or not helpful, and make clear what a student does that helps him work hard (is ready, quiet, attending, and when given seat work, pays attention to it, tries his hardest, and doesn't stop until he's finished). Desirable and undesirable behaviors could be listed under each rule.

Especially for the ADD child, I always make it clear what is meant by being polite to teachers, and by arguing with teachers. As an alternative to arguing, ways and times for bringing up and discussing viewpoints are outlined. I sometimes liken their situation to mine if I were speeding and caught by a police officer. I would be ill-advised to argue or be rude to her when she is giving me a ticket. Yet, if I believe I didn't break a rule I can have my day in court to explain this. However, I must appear at the time set by the court — not at my choosing.

I also make sure children understand that all adults working with a child are considered "teachers" and deserve the same courtesy and respect, whether these be aides or parent volunteers.

rewards
In a regular size class (including several "behavior problems") I have formed groups with a "behavior problem" in each and have recorded points on the chalkboard. In some grade one or two classes, students have responded well to a system where the only reward I used was the privilege of being dismissed first. During the time blocks between each break, I would keep track of points for each row. Then I would dismiss rows in the order of the points they had earned with about twenty to thirty seconds in between (of course, a row might miss it's turn if all students weren't ready). This reward worked amazingly well — better than small prizes. This seemed due not only to getting out thirty seconds before another group, but to the status involved in being dismissed earlier. Because there was a dismissal about every two hours, "prizes" were also quite immediate.

In a class of eight to ten students with learning and behavior problems, I have found poker chips to work well. Not only can they be quickly and quietly awarded and taken away, but they are a good size to keep in my pocket, and students like to handle them. We pretend the chips are money and thus, students are paid for good behavior and fined for bad. We also use them in learning to count money.

At the beginning of the year I tape a wide-mouthed plastic glass on the corner of each student's desk top. We normally use blue chips as nickles and white as dimes. Students start the day with eighty cents in their glasses, and the object is to have one dollar or more by noon. We start over after lunch.

When I award tokens, I make a point of commenting on the desirable behavior for all to hear. When I walk up to a student's desk and say, "I see you're keeping right on working without looking around" or, "I like the way you are ready to listen so quickly," as I put a chip into the glass, nearby students are immediately on task or ready to listen without my having to draw attention to their off-task behavior. Students are so interested in earning tokens and in keeping a running tally of how much "money" they have in their glasses, that I've had to make a rule about when they may be counted so students keep their minds on their work.

Fifteen minutes before lunch, we gather around each student's desk in turn, and they count their money. This gives valuable, regular practice in counting money by fives and tens as well as extra motivation to students. Those who have a dollar or more are congratulated, but those who don't are not put down. Rather, they are offered encouragement by statements such as, "too bad" and, "maybe tomorrow." I find if I at first make comments like this, students soon take over in encouraging each other.

Those who have "made it" are allowed ten minutes free time. Many activities of value in themselves such as games and puppets, computer, and listening centre are offered for free choice during this time. This time is also used for completion of work not finished and for handling problems that have come up during the morning. As well, it is a good time for observing social interaction and social skills of students. Some classrooms may not be able to afford two ten-minute blocks of free time every day. For my class, I feel that it saves me at least that amount of time in disciplining and keeps a positive atmosphere in the classroom.

penalties

For the most part, undesirable behavior is penalized by loss of one or more tokens. If necessary, I comment quietly, without drawing attention to the student, about the rule broken. Sometimes, however, misbehavior continues after the loss of one or more tokens, or a student argues or has a temper tantrum over losing tokens. In these cases we move on to a time-out procedure. I have a chair in a corner partly behind a door, but directly in my view, where the student must spend five minutes (more if he doesn't go directly to the chair). If there is noticeable movement or noise from the student, the timer is reset. Any child who attempts to communicate with the "time-out student" also serves five minutes on a nearby chair. I have found this system to usually work better than sending a child out of the room though there are occasions when a trip to the office by a child who will not settle down is necessary.

Contingency Contracting

Essentially a reward system that involves a written contract, contingency contracting can be a useful way to set up a program for one student. It is a particularly helpful way of dealing with older children or gifted children. It is a good way of targetting one particulaly bothersome behavior.

In setting up the contract, both the child and parents or teachers state what they would like from each other. Parents or teachers state the behavior or performance they want to see from the child and the child states what reward he would like in return. They then negotiate until they arrive at a satisfactory contract. Details of both the expected performance and the timing etc. for the reward are discussed and defined exactly so they are clear to everyone. Then a contract is written up in which the reward is contingent on the child displaying the desired behavior or performance. There may be partial or lesser rewards for partial performance. The contract is signed by the child and teachers or parents.

A school contract might read, "Each morning Jimmy is to complete in the time alloted all written assignments in a manner satisfactory to Mrs. Brown. He is to correct all mistakes on each assignment and to have these checked by Mrs. Brown. If he does this, he will be allowed to select a disk from those provided and use it on the computer between 11:50 a.m. and 11:57 a.m. that day."

A teacher might negotiate to allow a child to leave one correction undone as a way of giving him input into the quality of work required. One of the main advantages of using this technique is that it is more likely to gain student cooperation than a plan set up by the teacher alone. The more real input allowed from the student, the better. For the child turned off by school or hostile to other behavior management systems, this plan may work. Its particular aptness for gifted ADD students will be discussed in the next chapter. For the child with very low self-esteem, this plan has an advantage in that there are no penalties other than missing the reward if it is not earned. Children with very low self-esteem may tend to see penalties as another strike against them in an unfair world. The reward given here should generally be a tangible item or a special privilege desired by the child. The more immediate the reward the better, but it should be obtainable within a week.

Conclusion

Although a behavioral management system may not solve all of a parent's or teacher's problems with an ADD child, it can help keep a positive atmosphere in the home or classroom. Such a program may be all that is needed for some ADD children with mild behavioral problems. It can be very useful for children that have responded positively to medication, but still have difficulties. For some ADD children who do not respond to medication, a behavioral program can be the best intervention known at the moment. Even though the behavior of some children may show no long term change, parents and teachers will know they have dealt with misbehavior in a way that is preferable to trying to coerce these children into changing their behavior by yelling, threatening or frequent physical punishment.

8

Other Behavioral, Psychological and Educational Interventions:

What are Some Helpful Strategies?

In Chapter Six, Marla's parents used a variety of behavioral techniques, some of which will be discussed in this chapter. They also participated in counselling with a psychologist from the children's hospital and reported this to be extremely helpful to them in coming to terms with the problems they were facing. When Marla was a teen, she attended teen group sessions while her parents attended corresponding sessions for parents. The parents reported this as helpful in that they were able to talk to others who were having problems with their children, and said Marla, who had few friends, appeared to enjoy and gain some benefit from the teen group.

Counselling or Therapy for the Family

There are times when it can be extremely beneficial for the family of an ADD child or individual members to participate in some type of counselling or therapy. This might be in conjunction with setting up and monitoring behavioral interventions, but can deal with other important issues as well. In a group, individually, or as a couple, parents can attempt to understand the nature of ADD and their particular child's problems and work out a way of explaining this simply to others. They can deal with the reality that there are at present no totally satisfactory answers to ADD, and that they may continue to have difficulty with their child. They may come to terms with the fact that they can only do their best and that their child may not achieve all of the things they had hoped for him. They can look at the fears they may have for their child, fears such as his not finishing school or being able to hold a responsible job, fears he may injure himself or others in a moment of rashness — even fears he may end up in jail because of his impulsiveness and lack of forethought.

At the same time, they can look at the bright side of the picture. Their child, because of his abundant energy, may do very well in some fields. He may outgrow his problems completely or partially. They can look at treatments, strategies and other factors which are favorable toward a good outcome for their child even if he doesn't outgrow his problems.

To gain in empathy, they can look at problems from their child's point of view. How does it feel when you continually disappoint yourself and others? How does it feel to have few friends and constant problems concentrating and fulfilling expectations at school. Parents can learn to remind themselves and each other that the child is not purposely misbehaving to make their lives miserable. It's just very difficult for him to behave as they'd wish. Though it might not always be apparent, he does value and want his parents' approval. Ways can be sought to show this approval and reasonable expectations can be set up for the child.

Parents will likely benefit, as well, from discussions that bolster their self-esteem and their confidence as parents. These may be badly shaken, and a strong confident parent has the best chance of dealing successfully with an ADD child. Discussions can help them find their strengths as parents, as well as realize that blaming themselves or each other is non-productive and destructive.

It may be useful to include the ADD child and siblings in some sessions to get everyone's feelings and perceptions out into the open. Other children in the family may feel cheated because the ADD child recieves more attention than they and may be angry because of harassment or aggression from the ADD child. They may be embarrassed at school or in the community because of the ADD child. Various ways of dealing with these problems can be looked at. Problems and needs of families will vary and these are only a few of the issues that might be dealt with in counselling sessions.

Counselling for The ADD Child

Especially as the ADD child gets older, he is likely to have emotional problems, and can benefit greatly from counselling directed at his needs. He may see himself as dumb, unlikable and bad, and his self-concept and low self-esteem will likely need to be addressed. Social and family problems can be discussed and feelings addressed along with discussions and practice of useful approaches to dealing with these problems. Ways of dealing with anger and impulses can be explored and stress reduction and anger control through biofeedback, visualization, progressive relaxation or other techniques can be tried. Some psychologists offer help with strategies for organization and problem solving, as well as strategies for improving school work and study skills. Many can deal with vocational counselling and a variety of other needs that the ADD child may have.

Time-Out for Parents

Most parents, especially mothers at home with small children, will benefit from regular breaks from their children. For parents of ADD children this can be critical. Regular breaks during which parents can enjoy each other's company and socialize with other adults can help parents keep a sense of perspective and nurture their support for each other and their self-esteem. For a mother staying at home with an ADD child, it is also advisable to find some type of babysitting exchange or service which will allow for breaks from the child during the day. If parents can't afford or arrange other babysitting, they can spell off each other so that each can have some time away from the child. Some social service programs will provide limited care at minimal or no cost. These services may be a necessity for a single parent of an ADD child.

At times a break from the child may be necessary to prevent emotional or physical abuse of the child. A mother at home with small children, one or more of whom are ADD, may become overwhelmed with the pressure of constant demands and aversive behavior of the ADD child. A father or mother who has had a hard day at work may have little patience for a noisy, argumentative child who is climbing the walls and resists all attempts to settle him. Sometimes the best thing one can do is get some distance from the child. If there is someone to look after the child, getting out for a walk or other physical activity can help regain one's equilibrium.

If a parent is alone with small children and no babysitting is available, taking the children out for a change of scene and some activity for both parent and child can help. Go to a park or a swimming pool, or in the winter go out and build a snowman. At times when pressures are building and coercive behavior is starting to escalate, parents should learn to give themselves an inner signal that the time has come to interrupt the pattern and get away for some physical activity with or without the child. As mentioned, counselling can be invaluable in learning to recognize and deal with these feelings and in finding other ways to deal with the stress of parenting an ADD child.

Other Techniques and Considerations

A number of other procedures can encourage good self-eseem for the ADD child and keep matters on an even keel both at home and at school. The following will be elaborated on:

1. Letting the child know you like him.
2. Finding a quiet talking time.
3. Helping the child express his feelings.
4. Maintaining a fun time.
5. Finding something the child is good at.
6. Getting a pet.
7. Using a firm, confident approach.
8. Criticizing the behavior not the child.
9. Labelling behaviors.
10. Labelling job requirements.
11. Giving one — and only one warning.
12. "You can't do this until you've done that" technique.
13. Timing.
14. Cognitive behavior training.
15. Social skills training.

letting the child know you like him

Probably the most beneficial action you can take toward an ADD child is to let him know in unmistakable terms that you like him. The best way to do this seems to be to tell him so in words. You may show a child in all kinds of ways that you care, but it seems to be important for these children to hear the words sincerely spoken. From a parent it may be important for the child to know that you like him as well as love him. He may feel that as a parent you are "expected to" or "automatically" love him — not so with liking.

This means that you must find a time when he is open to listening to you, and when you genuinely feel you like him. One good time to do this can be after there has been a conflict and he has had time to cool down. At this point he will often feel remorseful or conciliatory. You can elaborate on some of the things you like about him such as his smile, his liveliness (some of the time), the caring attitude he shows at times and as many other things as come to mind. Because he is well aware that you don't like many of his behaviors, this should be mentioned too. As the ADD child is so often in trouble and genuinely feels persecuted, knowing someone genuinely likes him can be a real boost to his spirit. You will often find him trying harder, at least for a while. Once is not enough though — the ADD child seems to need affirmation at regular intervals that someone does indeed like him and will continue to like him.

finding a quiet talking time

Many years ago, a wise mother of an ADD adolescent shared with me what she felt was the most important thing she did for her son. This was arranging a quiet talking time with him each day, thus keeping open the lines of communication. At bedtime each night, she went to his room for a short chat with him about his day. It is sometimes hard to get the ADD child to voluntarily enter into a meaningful conversation. When he is settled into bed at night often seems the best time for parents to genuinely talk *with* him rather than *at* him. Teachers too, can try to find opportunities to talk as a friend to the ADD student.

helping the child express his feelings

When talking with an ADD child, it is often benificial to help him express his feelings, and have him realize that feelings in themselves aren't bad. It may be helpful to explain that everyone has "bad" feelings at times, but we try not to express them in action. He can be encouraged to tell parents when he is angry or upset and may be allowed certain ways of expressing this such as pounding a pillow or slamming his door.

maintaining a fun time with the child

Parents (and teachers when feasible) should try to maintain a "fun" time with the child — if possible sharing some of his interests. While many ADD children seem drawn to watching television, mimicking Ninjas, riding dirt bikes and the like, with effort, one can often find a sport or a pastime that is at least somewhat mutually interesting.

finding something the child is good at

Lucky is the ADD child who has a sport or hobby which has drawn his interest and in which he excels. Many times it is not that easy. Because some ADD children have coordination problems, they can have difficulty with sports. Yet, because they have difficulty with one sport doesn't mean they will have difficulty with all. There are some of these children, too, who do poorly at team sports, but do well at individual sports such as BMX racing, speed skating or swimming. If a child does not do well at sports, hobbies or groups such as cubs can be investigated. It may require some searching, but the results can be worth it. I know of one child with learning problems whose mom discovered he had a talent for building things, so she hired a carpenter to work with him in making a number of projects. The competence and the tangible products the child was able to show were a definite boost to his self-esteem.

buying a pet

A pet can offer unconditional love and attention to the ADD child, and these children often seem drawn to animals they can touch and handle. A pet doesn't usually object to being bossed, and will always be there when friends might not. Unfortunately, however, a pet may not be advisable for some ADD children, especially when they are younger if they have a tendency to be too rough and might abuse the animal. In some cases where this might be a problem, a meduim sized or larger dog may be a better choice than a guinea pig or a cat. In circumstances where it is feasible, a pet can often provide an important outlet for an ADD child.

maintaining a firm, confident approach

In dealing with the misbehavior of an ADD child, a reasoning approach usually doesn't work. Trying to talk him into behaving more acceptably is often a disaster because of his lack of control and penchant for arguing. Rather, the ADD child often responds best to firmness and a sense that an adult is in control and confident, as opposed to either an aggressive stance ("I'm going to make you.") or pleading stance ("Please be good.") on the part of an adult. It might be said that the best parent or teacher for an ADD child is like a turtle — firm on the outside, but soft on the inside. A parent or teacher who is feeling "stressed out" may have particular difficulty coping with an ADD child and maintaining a firm, consistent, friendly attitude. In such cases, it may be wise to seek stress management classes, counselling or other avenues directed toward stress reduction.

criticizing the behavior not the child

When teachers or parents must criticize a child, it is best if the criticism refers to the specific objectional behavior rather than to the child in general. It is much easier for the child to take, and less damaging to his self-esteem to say, "I don't like it when you hit your sister," rather than "Why are you always such a bad boy?" The first criticizes the behavior, the second criticizes the child.

labelling behaviors

Techniques that avoid giving a direct order can assist the ADD child who is extremely sensitive to criticism and flies into a verbal tantrum at the least frustration. A technique that may be useful in this regard is that of labelling. Rather than telling the child to stop a behavior, his undesirable behavior can be given a label and pointed out to him. If different behaviors he displays can be grouped under labels such as, "bugging" or "getting wound up," these labels can be used in pointing out to the child that he is doing something offensive. If the ADD child's behavior is calmly labelled along with a reminder of the consequences if he doesn't desist, this may help him gain control over his behavior better than will a direct order to stop.

labelling job requirements

A labelling technique can also be used to remind the child of something he needs to do. Rather than saying, "Do the dishes now," one can say, "The dishes are still on the table. Remember if they're not started within ten minutes you will have another job added to your list, and it will have to be done before you watch TV or go anywhere." This type of reminder, rather than a direct command, may be easier for the ADD child to respond to calmly. The use of a calm non-emotional voice is also important. An angry, excited voice changes a reminder into a threat — to which an ADD child will often respond explosively.

giving one and only one warning

In reminding the child of the consequences for his behavior, the child should be given one warning — but only one — before the consequence comes into effect. Research with ADD children has shown a better response if children are given a warning. However, if the child does not comply, the consequence must follow immediately, so the child learns that he will be reminded only once.

"You can't do this until you've done that" technique

A technique that can be useful in gaining a child's cooperation in doing a task is stating that: "You wont be able to do ___ until you've done ___," with the first blank being filled with something the child wants to do, and the second being filled with something a parent or teacher wants him to do. This is a kind of contingency command — the child's getting something is contigent on him doing something. Thus one might say, "You can't watch TV until you've taken out the garbage." Because an immediate reward hangs on the completion of the task, this technique is very effective, though short term. Routines can be set up this way as well — with rules that apply regularly such as, "You can't leave the kitchen until the dishes are done," or "On Mondays you can't eat supper until you've put away your clean clothes in your drawers and closet."

timing

When you have asked the child to do something and he is dragging his heels, counting to ten or using a stop watch can be very effective. At school, a stop watch, preferably somewhere where the child can glance at it, may provide incentive to keep on task. Often just the fact that he is being timed will urge on a child, but a penalty for not finishing within a given time can be added if necessary.

At school, some distractible children may work well if they are given a ten to fifteen minute block of work at a time. If they complete it on time, they can be allowed five minutes for free time or for an activity that appeals to them. If a child doesn't finish the work in the time given, he should be required to finish it at recess or during another fun activity. He should then go on to another block of work. In cases where a teacher or a volunteer parent are working individually with a child who is having difficulty keeping on task, incentive to pay attention can be provided by timing off task periods and having him make up the time. It usually doesn't take long for a child's attention to return when he sees the stop watch and knows what you are doing.

cognitive behavior training

Cognitive behavior training involves teaching the child to think about and monitor his own behavior. Children are taught to talk themselves through a series of steps when doing school work or dealing with social or other problems. Commercial programs are available for use in school classrooms, and some curriculum guides now recommend teaching students to monitor their learning by using a series of steps similar to those used in various cognitive training programs. After looking at a number of such programs, I have drawn out the following steps students can be taught, along with questions students can use to prompt themselves as they follow the steps.

1. Define the problem. (What do I need to do?)

2. Formulate plans of action. (What are some possible plans?)

3. Choose a plan. (Which plan shall I try first?)

4. Evaluate continuously. (Is the plan working? If not, do I need to concentrate more or do I need a different plan?)

5. Do a final evaluation. (How did I do? If very well, I should keep up the good work. If not, what can I change next time?)

Since 1970, such programs have been taught to ADD children in an attempt to help them control their own behavior as opposed to behavior modification where the control lies with the parent or teacher (Ingersoll 1988, 94). Unfortunately, while such programs seem a promising approach to the problems of the ADD child, research has shown little success in ADD children transferring these skills to the problems they deal with in real life. However, elements from these programs can be useful in some ways.

I have used both a commercial program called "Think Aloud" (B.W. Camp and M.A. Bash, 1985), and a program I simplified for use with ADD children and children with other learning problems. I found the commercial program — with steps similar to those outlined above — to be too detailed and complicated for young primary children to apply by themselves to either their school work or their interpersonal problems. However, I found the steps to be a useful model for me as a teacher to use when helping students with their school work.

The simplified program I use consists of two questions only: "What's the problem?" and "What's the plan?" While I saw only occasional indications that children were applying these steps without prompting, I found them useful steps to use in group problem solving.

Another technique I have found to help some ADD children is "Stop and Think." Here the teacher labels certain questions as "Stop and Think questions." Then, students are not allowed to put up their hands to answer until the teacher's hand goes up as a signal. When this technique is used, it helps ADD students to remember to raise their hands and some students give better answers.

social skills training

Poor impulse control and lack of awareness of social subtleties and others' feelings often lead to severe social problems for the ADD child. Although the use of cognitive behavior training for dealing with social problems has had little lasting success in helping the ADD child control impulses and "tune in" to other's feelings, the discussions that take place can raise the level of awareness of both the ADD child and his peers. It may be a very useful approach to use with an ADD child if his social problems continue once he has been placed on medication and has more self control.

As part of social skills training, it is helpful to discuss and role play various social situations. Topics of discussion might include nonverbal behavior, putting oneself in another's shoes, and recognizing the feelings of others. Parents, as well as teachers, can role play and discuss these issues with an ADD child. One mother drew a series of cartoons in which the main character (obviously an ADD individual) was shown displaying a variety of both desirable and undesirable behaviors. Then she talked to her ADD child about how others might feel about and respond to the various behaviors. She found the cartoons successful both in keeping her child's attention and helping him understand how his actions influenced others.

special consideration at school

Barbara Ingersoll, in her book *Your Hyperactive Child*, tells of interviews done with hyperactive teenagers and young adults by Doctors Gabrielle Weiss and Lily Hechtman at Montreal Children's Hospital (Ingersoll 1988, 159). When these ADD teenagers and young adults were asked to recall important events in their childhood, they often described very good relationships with certain teachers. In fact, some described their experiences with these teachers as turning points in their lives. Unfortunately, others recalled hurtful experiences with teachers whom they felt shamed them, made them feel dumb, and didn't like them. (This is not to say that the teachers purposely did this, but this was the perception of these young people.)

Ingersoll goes on to state that she has on numerous occasions seen a dramatic improvement in a hyperactive child's behavior, school work, self-esteem and general outlook on life when he has been placed with a teacher with whom he "clicks." She states that she has also seen many children take a sharp turn for the worse when placed with a teacher where the relationship is poor.

This is something I have observed as well. For some hyperactive children, the student-teacher match seems critical and can make a great deal of difference to the student's life. When a particular child and a particular teacher don't "click," it in no way reflects badly on the teacher. These can be very difficult children who get along poorly with many people. However, in cases like this, if there is another teacher with whom the relationship might be better, it is important that the child be moved if possible. It is also beneficial when those placing such children in classes are aware of the significance of student-teacher match and take this into account whenever possible.

There are those who say that children should learn to get along with all kinds of people as preparation for adulthood. In adulthood, though, we have a great deal more say in whom we associate with and work for than do children in school. As well, many ADD children improve as they get older and will later have a better chance of coping with all kinds of people. For any ADD child, a relatively successful school year can be important to his self-esteem and his life.

As students become older and become more responsible for turning in assignments on their own and for the quality and completeness of their work, it may be necessary for teachers to monitor the ADD student more closely than others. If assignments are not turned in or are incomplete, the teacher should inform parents right away to see if they are able to rectify this. In some cases it may work best to keep the student after class to finish assigned work.

Most teachers who have worked with highly distractible, inattentive students have found that seating such students at the front of the class or near the teacher is helpful. This cuts down the student's view of other potential distractions and helps focus attention on the teacher. There are a number of other teaching strategies that can help compensate for the learning problems experienced by many ADD children.

Teaching Techniques that Capture Interest and Aid Listening and Organizational Skills

Children with attentional difficulties, because their minds wander, often have problems taking in information through listening and in following oral instructions. There are a number of techniques which can help capture and hold the attention of such children, and at the same time bolster their poor listening skills. These are some of the same techniques often used with younger children and for children with learning difficulties who have problems in the area of listening. However, there is evidence that all children, and even adults, learn more efficiently if such techniques are used. I have watched a videotape of the computer monitored brain activity of an older student under various learning conditions. A small light blinked on and off on the computer screen showing the brain activity of this student listening to a teacher lecture. Yet the screen came alive with flashing lights indicating greatly increased brain activity as the individual became involved in multi-sensory learning. Techniques that combine other senses with auditory learning not only help ADD children and others learn more easily and retain longer what they have learned, they make the learning experience more enjoyable for everyone.

Some of these techniques do require extra preparation for an already busy teacher, and may not be feasible to attempt on a regular basis. Yet others, like visualization and role playing, once learned and kept in the front of the mind, require only a bit of creativity to fit into lesson plans or use in an impromptu fashion. Another consideration for a teacher trying to proceed through a curriculum in target time is the extra time some types of direct experience or multisensory lessons require. Obviously, some techniques will need to be saved for important or difficult concepts.

Visual techniques which can bolster learning include:
1. Using visual materials.
2. Using color
3. Flashlight tracking
4. Visualization and fantasy
5. Using metaphor.

using visual materials

Teachers and designers of educational materials know of the effectiveness of pictures, films, maps and charts etc. in helping children to understand and remember information and concepts. As well, most teachers add emphasis to important ideas by writing them on the chalkboard. Yet, visual images could be used more consistently in teaching, and words could be translated to pictures or other visual forms more often. Many concepts could be sketched as a teacher talked. Though stick figures and crude drawings might have to suffice, this could provide a useful visual element to aid in understanding and holding attention.

Webbing (also called clustering or mapping), often used in brain storming activities, could be used in notes written on the board for children to copy. This technique illustrates the relationship between ideas more concretely than does paragraphing and provides a stronger visual element than printed words alone. The technique of webbing can be a valuable one to teach ADD and other students to use for outlining or organizing their prewriting, and is á good alternate form in which to allow students to present their written assignments. It can make writing more like talking pictures and can be helpful to ADD students in organizing their thoughts and work. It will be helpful to all students who prefer simultaneous learning (starting from the whole and moving into the parts or seeing the whole picture rather than the parts). Later in this chapter, webbing is used to illustrate and explain various types of direct experience learning that can be helpful to the ADD child and others.

Much of what we teach in school is taught sequentially or moving step by step, but this way of learning may be difficult for a student with attentional difficulties. Strong simultaneous learners, who may or may not be ADD, frequently find this step by step process frustrating as they wait for the teacher to finally get to the point, which these students often see immediately once they are given the whole picture. Strong simultaneous learners tend to see everything at once in their minds and some type of visual representation can be very important to them. Simultaneous learners, will often benefit from seeing a finished product or a finished picture before they are taken through the steps leading to the product. Show them a completed craft, carving, or art product before they begin or go through an experiment or math problem, and get to the result quickly before doing the slow step by step lesson.

color

Purposeful use of color can aid organizational skills and add interest to lessons. ADD students who have trouble organizing their desks and materials can use color coding to mark materials that go with one subject or belong in one area. Students can color the spines of scribblers the dominant color for the text that goes with that subject or according to a predetermined code or, for easy locating, can mark all items that go in one area of their desks with a specific color. Materials can be put away in their color areas and quickly located by looking at the color on the spine of the book or markings on other materials.

Teachers can use different colored chalks or felts to add interest or to emphasize the organization of notes the children are to read and/or copy. For younger children the first word in each sentence can be green for go and the last, red for stop. Progress in copying notes can be seen and felt more easily if each sentence or paragraph is written in a different color (this also helps students who have difficulty finding their place).

flashlight tracking

Using a flashlight as a pointer in a partially darkened room can add interest and help keep student's attention where you want it. You can follow a line of print or arithmetic problems with a flashlight. You can also outline on the chalkboard or ceiling letters, numbers or words you want the children to learn. For counting or adding, you can use flashes of light for the students to count.

visualization and fantasy

Visualization or fantasy can transform an ordinary lesson into an exciting adventure. Children fantasize naturally (this is a skill that may be well developed in the ADD child), so teachers may as well take advantage of this powerful and useful process. A lesson on the metamorphosis of a butterfly can be made much more meaningful and interesting if children visualize themselves as the caterpillar foraging for food and so on. Visualization can be a powerful way to encourage comprehension in reading or to review a happening in social studies such as the settling of the West. Visualization need not be realistic, but can become pure fantasy. Students can make a visual image of such concepts as a fraction, a verb, a town or infinity. They can make a visual image of a molecule of water freezing as they study this process or of a white blood cell attacking bacteria, and to add interest and consolidate learning, they can be asked to draw the image they fantasized. The book, *Put Your Mother on the Ceiling: Children's Imagination Games* (DeMille 1973), explains visualization more fully and provides a model for visualization exercises with children.

metaphor

Teachers already use metaphor — whenever they compare one thing or process to another and point out how they are alike. Not strictly visual, metaphors, nevertheless, compare something complete to something else complete and lend themselves to visual representation. Teachers are using metaphor when they compare electricity moving through wiring to water running through pipes, and when they compare floating seeds to parachutes, and seeds that stick to velcro. Students are helped to understand new processes by having them compared to familiar processes, and a real object or a diagram can be an aid to interest and retention. Metaphor can be used much more extensively than it is presently used, and students can be challenged to come up with their own metaphors to demonstrate understanding. An excellent and thorough discussion of metaphor and how to enhance learning by teaching students to generate metaphors can be found in the book *Teaching for the Two-sided Mind: A Guide to Right Brain/Left Brain Education* (Williams 1983).

tactile and kinesthetic learning

Haptic or tactile learning refers to learning using the sense of touch, while kinesthetic learning refers to feeling movement or other sensations as a way of aiding learning. Both of these can add another dimension to learning and thus aid in holding interest and encouraging learning, particularly for the ADD child. Various haptic/kinesthetic techniques are explained in the following paragraphs.

"Tactile tracing" and "on body drawing" involve enhancing learning with the sense of touch. In the first of these methods, students learn letters, numbers, words or other symbols by tracing over a model made of sandpaper or other rough, raised surface at the same time they are hearing and/or saying the word, letter, etc. At times, students may simply trace on their desks or on paper with their fingers and this will help hold their attention and give them a tactile input to learning. For "on body drawing," students have words, numbers, letters or other symbols drawn on their backs between the shoulder blades, on the back of the hand or on their cheek. The teacher may do this or students may take turns drawing on each other. This can be used for learning spelling words or important lists.

"Air writing," "movement answers," and "crawling over figures" involve using a kinesthetic body movement while learning what is heard and/or seen. "Air writing" involves tracing words, letters, addition problems, etc., in the air using large enough movements that a shoulder movement (large muscle) is involved. This can be done with eyes closed to focus on the kinesthetic sensation. "Movement answers" involves doing something physical to signal an answer or to give a signal that one knows the answer. Thus, students may take one jump for yes, two for no or stand up and turn around if they know an answer. As well, in "crawling over figures," students may crawl over large letters or numbers on cardboard or outlined on the floor with masking tape letters, or may make a human clock using masking tape for a circle and children for the numbers and hands on the clock. As different times are called out, the hands move appropriately.

Some students will learn better if they are allowed to "jump and learn" sight words, spelling words or times tables, or if they have a short period of jumping just before they attempt learning such rote facts. Some will learn better if music and rhythmic movement are used while learning these same types of materials or if the words, etc., are chanted. Many children, even in the higher grades, will do better in math and other subjects if manipulative materials or objects they can handle are used as they learn concepts.

direct experience

Sometimes called concrete or multisensory learning this involves using all, or nearly all senses at once. This kind of learning includes:

1. Scientific experiments.
2. Real objects.
3. Field trips.
4. Simulation and role playing.

These methods are illustrated and explained in Figure 1 using webbing, a versatile, visual technique described earlier.

Additional Methods

This listing is far from exhaustive. It gives only a sampling of the type of activities and strategies that can augment listening and enhance learning for ADD and other students. During such activities, some ADD students will require a high degree of structure and direction. For some activities, teacher input and control will need to be maintained throughout the activity. At other times when students are to accomplish a task on their own, expectations will need to be clear as to exactly what students are to do and the amount of time they have in which to accomplish it. Students who get carried away when active participation is used may have to sit out for a time. Teachers will have to work out a balance between control and active participation for particular students. This is true as well when using cooperative learning and other interactive techniques where students discuss information and issues with each other, work together, and move about the room. These techniques may work well for some ADD students but not for others, depending on whether a teacher is able to find ways to effectively monitor and direct these students.

Two other methods that can be particularly effective with some ADD students are using a game approach and computer learning. Making a lesson into a game where team points are given for proper participation and effort will often appeal to the

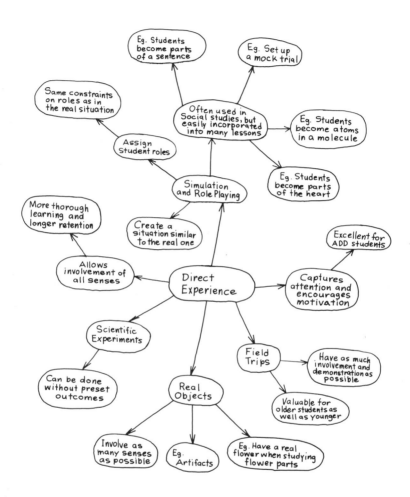

Figure 1

competitive side of the ADD child and result in high involvement. Usually points will need to be subtracted for calling out or poor sportsmanship, and the ADD child's team must win some of the time. As well, something as simple as getting to add a block to a tower or a part to a funny diagram for correct participation will often motivate and direct attention even if there is no competitive element (there are no teams).

Just as many ADD students perform better in a one to one situation, so do some of these same students become very involved in computer learning. Not only do they receive constant one to one attention and the chance to answer every question, they get to use physical movement in their responses. Obviously, neither of the above two methods can be used constantly, but they can be very helpful in assuring attention when important new concepts are taught and in making routine practice and review more palatable for the ADD student (and many others).

Special Placement

In spite of modification of classroom structure and teaching methods, along with other treatments and interventions, some ADD students will still show considerable underachievement. For these students, placement in a smaller size class with specific individualized methods is another alternative which may help the child achieve more satisfactorily, and give him a better opportunity to work on his social skills.

Conclusion

Counselling may be extremely useful for ADD children, and for their parents or siblings, to help deal with some of the issues that arise in the family due to the ADD. Participation in counselling does not mean that a parent is weak or deficient. An ADD child is likely to cause extreme stresses in a family, and he is a child who requires extra-special parenting. Regular breaks from the child are desirable for all parents of ADD children, and there may be circumstances where these are crucial.

There are a number of behavioral techniques that can bolster the ADD child's self-esteem both at home and at school. Though cognitive behavior training systems have proved disappointing as a means to help ADD children learn to deal with social and other problems, there are elements of these systems which can be helpful. Many teaching techniques can assist learning for the ADD child and others. These techniques hold attention and add visual, tactile/kinesthetic, and other sensory input to auditory input. Students then don't have to rely so heavily on listening (an area in which many ADD children have difficulty). Some of these techniques can also improve the ADD child's poor organizational skills. The teacher will need to maintain stucture and direction during many of these techniques. For some students, placement in a low-enrollment class with individualized methods may be needed.

9

The Gifted Student and ADD:

What are the Special Considerations?

Chad, a grade six student, scored high on intelligence and achievement tests, but his day to day school work left much to be desired. Doing anything that required sustained attention and organization, as do most written assignments, Chad needed considerable teacher supervision and encouragement and, even then, met only minimal requirements. He attempted to use his superior reasoning abilities to manipulate his teachers as he explained that he couldn't see the point in doing something he already knew how to do. Teachers, however, did not accept his view that if he could write one sentence he could write a whole page of them, or that if he knew the information about a topic he had no need to record it.

Other students saw him as low in ability and couldn't understand why he was allowed to participate in a gifted program. They had numerous complaints about Chad's behavior. They said he was always wiggling or moving around; he distracted them with his noise and disruptions; he used sarcasm and name calling on them, and he had a "know-it-all" attitude. Though teachers were exasperated in trying to get him to do better written work, most liked Chad and found his oral participation exceptional in terms of his background of knowledge and the creative solutions he proposed to problems. Yet because of what he produced, his marks had slipped as he progressed through school.

At home, his mother had found him a handful since he was two-years-old. She knew he was a good kid, but found she constantly had to keep on top of him. She explained that if she tried to use reasoning with him, he could present arguments that would impress a supreme court justice, so she often had to let him know in no uncertain terms who was boss.

Chad showed some of the special problems of the ADD-gifted child. Unlike many, though, he had been identified through individual testing and placed in a gifted program. Here he was labelled as a gifted underachiever and interventions recommended for such students were tried. However, even in the gifted program he continued to show exceptional abilities orally but produced little when sustained attention and organization were required.

Defining Giftedness

Gifted students are generally believed to constitute from 3 to 5 percent of the student population. There have been articles, chapters and books written in attempts to define giftedness. Yet the debate continues over what characteristics should be looked at in choosing students for gifted programs.

Most commonly, gifted students are defined as those who have potential or demonstrated ability for exceptional achievement. Consequently, it is felt that such students may require special programming to meet their needs and realize their potential. Most gifted programs use a multi-criteria selection process in identifying candidates for their gifted programs. Procedures may include intelligence testing, achievement testing and review of school marks; creativity testing, teacher, parent, and peer nomination, and looking at examples of exceptional projects these children have done.

Intelligence Scores as Criteria

Many gifted programs automatically include students who achieve above a certain score on an intelligence test — for example, those who score in the Very Superior range (IQ above 130) on the WISC-R (Wechsler Intelligence Scale for Children — Revised). For students who do not place above the IQ cut-off line, intelligence scores are still a primary criteria used in selection. However, ADD children who have the potential to score in the "gifted range" on an intelligence test may not do so because of their impulsivity and distractibility.

Russell Barkley, in a review of the literature on ADD in *Handbook of Clinical and Behavior Therapy with Children* (1985), points out research showing that ADD children frequently show a characteristic pattern on the WISC-R known as the "ACID profile." This means that ADD children often do poorly on specific subtests of the WISC-R — these subtests being: Arithmetic, Coding, Information and Digit Span (Barkley 1985, 170). It is believed these subtests are susceptible to attentional difficulties.

If it is possible to improve attention and concentration by use of medication or other means, then it would follow that these interventions should improve the IQ scores of these students. This is what happened in the case of Gary who was first tested before his ADD was somewhat controlled by medication. Although on initial testing he did well on the Information and Comprehension subtests of the WISC-R and was within the gifted range on tests measuring reasoning and thinking skills, Gary's score on the Arithmetic subtest was considerably below the average range and his score on Digit Span was very low as well. According to the examiner, this seemed not because Gary didn't understand concepts involved, but because he couldn't focus and concentrate well enough to remember and do all the steps on these two tests in their required order (questions were given orally and not repeated).

Retested with the same test about a year and one half later — after he had been on stimulant medication for five months — Gary's improvement was dramatic. His Arithmetic score shot up from well below average to the bright range and his Digit Span score came up to the average range. There was some change in other scores as well. His overall IQ score rose to the gifted range. This is merely one case and, certainly, generalizations can not be drawn from it in terms of treatment raising IQ scores. There are many other reasons a child might achieve better on an IQ test on one occasion than another. The psychologists involved, however, believed that Gary was putting forth his best effort on both occasions and that the scores achieved were an indication of his ability level at the time. As well, the rise in IQ score was coincidental with a similarly dramatic rise in Gary's school marks. This makes sense in that IQ marks are a general gauge of how well a student will do in school — barring factors such as learning disabilities.

Gary's case illustrates the possibility that students with reasoning and thinking ability comparable to children in gifted programs may not be considered for these programs because their overall IQ score is depressed by their attentional problems. Neither do these students generally perform well enough in school for teachers or peers to recommend them for gifted programs.

Other Criteria Used to Identify Gifted Students

Looking at the checklists which teachers, peers and parents use to recommend students for gifted programs, one often finds criterion that automatically disqualify ADD students from gifted programs. The Revolving Door Model for gifted programs was originated by an expert in the area of gifted education, Joseph Renzulli, Professor of Educational Psychology and Associate Director of the Bureau of Educational Research at the University of Connecticut. It is a model widely used in developing gifted programs. While this plan does provide enrichment for a wide variety of students, it identifies participants for gifted (Type III) programming by three general criteria: intellectual ability, creative ability, and task commitment (Renzulli 1977, 33-35). To be considered for higher level programming (Type III activities) students must show a high level of all three characteristics. While in spite of attentional handicaps, some ADD students will show high intelligence test results, and many will show a penchant for creativity, task commitment is a stumbling block for ADD students in gaining admission to these programs. High task commitment assumes strong focusing and concentration skills. It requires sticking to a project until one has done a thorough and excellent job of it. These are abilities ADD students seldom show.

Many other programs use teacher checklists with selection criteria such as: persistent goal directed behavior, requires little direction from the teacher, and works well independently. While such checklists are generally comprehensive, and it is not expected that students will meet all criteria, teachers often believe these particular criteria to be very important.

Joanne R. Whitmore, Ph.D., Assistant Dean for Teacher Education at Kent State University, in an article titled *Gifted Children with Handicapping Conditions: A New Frontier*, points out that most tests used to identify gifted children are normed on nonhandicapped populations. She goes on to state that "more reliable and valid instruments for identifying potential rather than just demonstrated ability to learn must be developed to allow early intervention with gifted/handicapped children." In outlining characteristics that impede identification of gifted/handicapped children, she notes that some children with disordered behavior, including aggressive, disruptive and frequent off-task conduct, are not identified. Characteristics that reveal giftedness in such children — but often go unheeded — include superior verbal skill, exceptional capacity for manipulating people and solving problems, and superior memory and general knowledge.

So it would seem that for several reasons, the gifted ADD student may fall outside of the net of the selection process for gifted programs. This may be due to attentional problems which depress intelligence test scores and achievement, or program designs which include high task commitment as an entry criteria, and or general misconceptions about the diverse nature of gifted individuals.

Gifted Underachievers

There are, however, many programs which adjust identification procedures in an attempt to find those gifted students who may not be showing their giftedness. Some feel these are the students who might benefit most if individual programming could meet their needs. These children have been labelled gifted underachievers and considerable research and effort has been directed toward finding the cause of, and solutions to, their problems.

When looking for causes of underachievement most often the home and school environments have been examined. As well, the high ability level of these students has been seen as instrumental in their underachievement: it has been suggested that because school work is too easy they have become bored and lost interest. These students' problems have been labelled in relation to their giftedness (i.e., gifted underachievers). Few have looked at other attributes of the students. Rarely has anyone looked at the temperament of the student as possibly involved in the underachievement. Interventions attempting to help these students at school have been generally unsuccessful (Colangelo and Dowdall 1982).

Finding little success in solving these students' problems at school, researchers have looked to the home as the source of the problems. In an article in the Spring 1988 issue of *The Gifted Child Quarterly*, three researchers in the area of gifted underachievement, Katherine Green, Marvin J. Fine, and Nona Tollefson, state that "underachievement is currently seen as a complex phenomena that is a manifestation of the interaction among family members and situational demands." These researchers examined differences in the functioning of families of gifted achievers and families of gifted underachievers. They were attempting to find variables in the families of underachievers that might be instrumental in the underachievment.

Their study included forty-five achieving gifted adolescent males and forty-five underachieving gifted adolescent males and the families of each. It was found that over two-thirds of the families of both achieving and underachieving gifted students were dysfunctional, and this was attributed to the fact that adolescence is a time of high family dysfunctionality. Interestingly, in this study only eight of the families of achieving gifted students came out as functional, while the families of underachieving gifted students did better in that ten of them rated as functional.

Though the researchers stated that "the speculation that underachievement may be more characteristic of families identified as dysfuncitonal than of families identified as functional was not supported" (Green, Fine, and Tollefson, 271), they went on to speculate about the reasons their theory had not been supported. Presenting no evidence to substantiate that such was the case, they reasoned that the families of the gifted achievers may have been experiencing temporary dysfunction due to the fact that their child was a teenager. On the other hand, they suggested that families of the underachieving gifted, may have been dysfunctional all along and it was coincidental that their child was now a teenager. This suggests a bias toward a conclusion that underachievement in the gifted is caused by family problems.

Perhaps the reason researchers have had difficulty in finding answers to the problems of the underachieving gifted is because — at least in some cases — they are looking in the wrong place. While the literature on ADD often mentions that some ADD children are gifted, and that these children will usually be underachievers, I have seen no reference to ADD in the literature on gifted underachievers. While it has been realized recently that gifted learners may have specific learning disabilities — generally in reading and/or math — it does not seem to have been realized that some may have ADD.

In looking at the literature on gifted underachievers it is interesting to note the characteristics listed to describe these children. Dowdall and Colangelo list the following traits: social immaturity, emotional problems, antisocial behavior and low self-concept. They also point out that in the population of gifted underachievers, males outnumber females two to one (Colangelo and Dowdall 1982).

Other descriptions of gifted underachievers include such characteristics as poor or uneven achievement, daily work consistently incomplete or poorly done, gap between oral and written work, aggressive in and out of the classroom, doesn't function well in a group; difficulty with peer relationships, few friends, dislikes practice work or drill, easily distractible; unable to concentrate and focus, inability to persevere, negative attitude toward school, and resistant to teacher efforts to discipline. It has also been observed that underachievement and adjustment difficulties tend to increase as the child proceeds through school. As I'm sure the reader will have noted, these characteristics described by Dowdall and Colangelo and others can also be indicative of ADD.

Other experts have listed different types of gifted students and suggested various techniques that might be useful for each type of student. George T. Betts of the University of Northern Colorado and Maureen Neilhart a doctoral student at the same university have recently portrayed five types of gifted and talented students explaining that "all gifted children are not affected by their special abilities in the same way." (Betts & Neihart 1988, 248). Of particular interest to this discussion are the Type II student, the Type IV student, and the Type V student that they describe. It is possible ADD students may be hidden in all three of these groups.

The Type II student they call the "challenging gifted." The feelings and attitudes they outline for this type include boredom, frustration, low self-esteem, impatience, defensiveness, heightened sensitivity and uncertainity about social roles. The behaviors they see this student exhibiting are correcting the teacher, questioning rules and policies, honesty and directness, mood swings, inconsistent work habits, poor self control, creativity, preference for active questioning approach, standing up for rights, and competitiveness. The authors state that these students are often perceived by peers and teachers as rebellious, engaged in a power struggle, and as discipline problems. They are often not seen as gifted (though this shows up in testing).

Type IV students, the "dropouts," are often a later version of Type II, and for the most part are high school students. They are perceived as feeling angry and rejected and show their feelings in either acting out or depression and withdrawal.

The Type V students of Betts and Neilhart are the "double labelled." It is recognized that some of these have learning disabilities or physical handicaps. Others are seen to be emotionally handicapped (as ADD students are often seen). These students show sloppy handwriting, and disruptive behaviors and seem discouraged, frustrated, rejected, helpless or isolated.

The interventions recommended to help these students are similar to many of the psychological interventions that have been tried with ADD children. They include such things as family counselling, individual counselling, placement with an appropriate teacher, cognitive and social skill development programs, activities to build self-esteem and behavioral contracting.

Underachievement Related to Giftedness

In descriptions of gifted underachievers, traits that show giftedness are listed along with traits related to underachievement. Because of this, the gifted underachiever is seen as an entirely different species of underachiever. There is little indication in the literature of attempts to relate the underachievement of gifted children to the underachievement of children in general. While it is true gifted students will have some problems and possiblities that are different, there is usefulness in looking at the literature on underachievement as it relates to ADD.

While ADD goes largely undetected in the general population of students, and the child's symptoms are usually blamed on the environment, this seems more so for the gifted. This happens because the underachievement and other problems these children have is generally seen to be related to their giftedness. Their inattention and restlessness is related to the fact that they are bored because the material is too easy for them. Yet in some cases, though these students may have advanced thinking skills they will have missed important learnings in school and truly don't know the material. As well, as noted earlier, the general feeling of ADD children in trying to cope with the step by step pace of school, is one of boredom or disinterest — whether or not they know a concept being taught. Because the gifted have advanced abilities, we tend to see their cases differently.

For gifted children, difficulties in getting along with peers is often thought to be due to their brightness which makes them feel "different" and to the fact that they perceive things more quickly and deeply than do other students. Yet the type of behaviors some of them display with their peer group are very similar to that of ADD children. They want to be the boss. They want things done their way and they want to win. Many, too, are impulsive and aggressive.

While many of the behavioral recommendations for the underachieving gifted are noticeably similar to the behavioral interventions mentioned for ADD students, some children would probably benefit more if their ADD were recognized. The search for a cause of the underachievement has been pretty well confined to examining the environment. Some of these children would likely benefit from having a doctor assess their problems. Yet there might be a reluctance to consider medication for such bright children in order to help them learn. However, the literature indicates that, for the most part, psychological and other interventions have been unsuccessful with these children (as they have with many ADD children).

If one considers again the possibility of an insufficiency of chemical transmitters in the brain (which it appears, is unrelated to intelligence), it becomes apparent that the abilities of these children can be just as imprisoned as those of children with less intellectual capabilities. And it is not just to aid their learning that help is imperative for some of these children. It is to help them with their lives.

Though figures vary from report to report, it is generally accepted that at least ten to fifteen percent of those identified as gifted have substantial difficulties including underachievement (Green, Fine and Tollefson 1988, 267). As mentioned, boys outnumber girls in a two to one ratio here. Some of these students drop out of school, some end up in jail and some commit suicide. These are grave problems and command serious consideration of all the evidence and possible interventions. This may require that the problems of these children be seen as more pervasive than as an off-shoot of their giftedness. This is not to deny that their giftedness will impact on the manifestation and solutions to their problems. Nor is it to say that all of these children are ADD, but it is likely that some of them are.

Recent reports in gifted literature are coming closer to understanding that the learning and social problems some gifted students present are not necessarily related to giftedness. Nicholas T. Gallucci, staff psychologist at the Institute of Living looked at the question of whether gifted children were prone to behavior problems related to their giftedness. (Galluci 1988, 273-275). Using a checklist commonly used to identify behavior problems — including those associated with ADD — he found that gifted children were essentially similar to children of average intelligence in the rate they showed problems on these measures. He concluded that the behavior problems of gifted children, "should be considered evidence of actual psychopathology rather than a result of giftedness."

This is consistent with what I have seen. Though their intellectual capabilities need to be taken into account, some of these children would likely benefit from treatment and intervention specific to their ADD. Gifted underachiever is a more prestigious label than ADD and perhaps, should be maintained if it will boost the self-esteem of affected students, but there needs to be recognition of the ADD to facilitate the most effective interventions.

Unfortunately, even if labelled gifted and included in gifted programs, many of these children see themselves as dumb. Mark, a highly gifted (in terms of tested intellectual ability) grade five ADD student, illustrates the perception these students often have of their abilities. Though bright, he was achieving poorly both in the classroom and in the gifted program when it came to written and other assignments which required focusing and sustained attention. Although he was allowed to choose any topic in which he was interested, and the gifted program teacher spent considerable time ferreting out his interest areas and allowed him a wide range of choice in the products he might make, she still spent a great deal of time keeping Mark on task. Though his knowledge of many areas was exceptional, he had difficulty focusing himself to take notes or make anything (even a poster or a model).

He had the problems with other students that are typical of ADD children. Even those in the gifted program didn't see him as bright. In an effort to deal with the perception of other students in the gifted program — who ostracized Mark — and to try and help him with self acceptance, the gifted program teacher held a discussion about ability levels and school achievement. She pointed out that some very bright students with exceptional abilities in some areas did poorly in school, and that there are qualities other than intelligence important to school success. The group discussed the fact that all students — including the gifted — have strengths and weaknesses. Mark showed an unfortunate interpretation of this discussion when he returned to the classroom and told his classroom teacher that he was gifted — but not smart.

The Impact of Giftedness on ADD

ADD children who are also gifted may have some problems accentuated. Both ADD children and gifted children often feel "different" from other students. The student who is both ADD and gifted will likely feel this difference more strongly. Both are sometimes seen as "know-it-alls" — the ADD student because of his temperament, the gifted student because he often perceives more deeply and quickly. The need to be right and to be the boss, added to the superior thinking ability and knowledge of the gifted student, may cause considerable resentment from peers who tend to resent both the dominating attitude and the superior knowledge.

Gifted programs challenge gifted students and allow them to mix with others like themselves to find natural friendships. Unfortunately, even within the gifted group, ADD students are often social outcasts. Gifted students notice the disabilities of the ADD child and, as in Mark's case, don't usually see these students as smart. Nor do they tolerate their offensive behavior any better than do other students. If the ADD-gifted student encounters another ADD-gifted student, the two will often compete and show little sensitivity toward each other, as sensitivity toward others is generally a quality in which ADD students are deficient.

ADD students who are gifted may have special problems with authority figures as well. If ADD-gifted children have good verbal skills they may be particularly adept at arguing and in trying to manipulate others. Being egocentric and defensive, their arguments may, nevertheless, be in many ways accurate, and be particularly unappreciated because of this. Their noting of detail and their strong insight may make them particularly able to perceive hypocrisy on the part of adults. They may note that they are punished for yelling, yet adults yell at them. They may see that we tell them to be fair, yet adults are often unfair to children (such as when both parties to a fight are punished, though one child may have been merely trying to ward-off the aggressor). They may note that they were punished when the teacher saw them pushing in line, yet they are not allowed to report on those who push them. They will likely see that they are in trouble more often than others, and this will add to their feelings of persecution.

As they grow older and their self-esteem lowers, if they commit antisocial acts such as lying and stealing, their superior intelligence will allow them to manipulate and deceive others to a greater degree than can less intelligent children. Thus, they may engage in such behavior for a longer time and to a more serious extent before they are discovered, and, in fact, they may not be caught.

If their brightness is obvious, their academic difficulties may have brought more criticism from adults than that experienced by less able children. Often they will lack self-confidence and feel they are dumb. At the same time, they will suffer the extreme frustration inherent in having exceptional abilities, yet not being able to actualize them — the agony of a bright mind locked within a disability.

Interventions for ADD-Gifted Children

Many of the interventions for these children will be similar to those for other ADD children. Because of their superior intellect, individual counselling may be particularly helpful to some of them. For some, though, this may not be effective unless they are placed on medication which can give them a different perspective on the world. Without medication they may be determined to side-track counselling and will often be able to do so. They may be determined that no one will manipulate them and see all attempts to help them in this light. Similarly, they may be adept at derailing behavior modification programs if they see these as a power struggle. Medication may be able to alleviate the feeling they have that the world is against them. Then they will more likely benefit from such a program.

For these particular ADD children it seems important to get their cooperation and participation in all interventions. This is why contingency contracting which involves student input and signing of the behavior management plan is often suggested for these children. If one can gain their cooperation, they are often quite capable of outlining conditions under which they work best and rewards and consequences that would be most effective for them. Because of their obvious ability to reason and discuss plans, one may think they should be able to carry out plans and monitor themselves as well. However, they seem to need an adult to monitor and administer both positive and negative consequences to the same extent that less intellectually capable students do.

In spite of their various misbehaviors, these children are often appealing — to some adults at least — because of their insight, and because they often have a side to them (as do many ADD youngsters) that adults find engaging. Luckily, in an attempt to reach the sometimes obvious potential of these children, some adults will spend extra time and effort on them. As was mentioned in the last chapter, it can be a real lifesaver for these students when they find an adult with whom they "click." If the ADD-gifted child can find someone he admires who understands (or tolerates) his difficulties and believes in his possibilities, he is indeed a lucky child. If the two relate well and share an interest, this person may serve as a mentor to the child. Because of their advanced thinking abilities and broad interests, with encouragement, some of these children can do very well in an area in which they are interested. This may be in a hobby or in a school subject such as science or electronics. Unfortunately, though many adults may be keenly interested in helping such a child (and this will undoubtedly be of some benefit), it is not always possible to cultivate the "magic" of a special relationship.

One of the things that may be overlooked for the ADD-gifted child is the need for remedial work in some areas. Because he is so bright, we sometimes overlook the fact that he may be weak in some important skills. To the extent possible, it is important to find stimulating and interesting ways for him to catch up in weak areas. He may not need a lot of drill and repetition, but he will need to be kept interested.

Because he will likely have some learning strengths, teachers should capitalize on these when possible. Like many other ADD students, he may be weak in listening skills. In this case, the teacher can provide pictures and other visual aids as for other ADD students with these problems. The ADD-gifted student may be particularly good at visualization, fantasy and metaphor. A "mapping"or "webbing"approach to organizing his work may be particularly useful.

Conclusion

Many ADD-gifted students will not gain admittance to gifted programs because attentional problems pull down test scores, because they fail to show their brightness in school work, and because the criteria for admittance to some such programs automatically excludes them. Those ADD children who are identified as gifted will often have their ADD symptoms seen as caused by or in relation to their giftedness. This may prevent them from getting the type of help they need. Such students are usually labelled as gifted underachievers.

Interventions for these students are essentially similar to interventions for all ADD students. However, success with these students often relies more heavily on gaining their cooperation, as they seem to have a strong need for input and are especially capable in sabotaging attempts to deal with them. Medication may be as essential for these students as for less capable students, and some will show little improvement in diverse areas of their lives without it. As in the case of other ADD students, a "special" adult may change their lives and — especially for these capable students — that important adult may be a mentor.

10

ADD and Adulthood:

What is the outlook?

Jay's case was described in the introduction to this book. His ADD difficulties — along with problems secondary to the frustrations and failures he suffered — extended into adulthood. At the time of Jay's childhood and school experience, little was known about the cause of ADD. It was widely assumed that problems like Jay's were the result of poor parenting. Learning disabilities weren't yet recognized, nor was the impact of ADD on school achievement and adjustment. Poor school performance was seen to be due to poor motivation.

Though Jay came from a working class family with strong family values, where parenting methods worked well with other children in the family, he showed himself to be different from his two brothers before he entered school. Yet the family knew of no resources that might be helpful in dealing with him. They did not see his problems as possibly medical, nor did they know of potentially helpful psychological resources in the community (and perhaps there weren't any at the time). Had they known of resources that might aid them, it is unlikely they would have sought help, because Jay's was a family (like many others) that felt such problems were private and should be handled within the family. Although as Jay grew older there was much family strife, they did not seek help.

In comparison, we can look at Gary, mentioned in the last chapter. Gary is not yet finished high school, but is achieving reasonably well and has made plans for further career training once finished school.

The overall intellectual ability of the two boys was similar if one looks at Gary's scores before medication. However, by junior high school, Jay's reading ability was considerably below grade level while Gary's was at grade level. It is quite likely that Jay had learning disabilities as well as ADD. Although Gary under-achieved considerably and disliked school, he was generally able to keep his marks at grade level and did not experience the degree of failure that Jay did.

On the other hand, Gary, as a preschooler, got into far more trouble due to his bossiness and aggressiveness than did Jay, though both were rejected by peers during elementary school. Yet, by junior high school, Jay was considerably more alienated from the mainstream of his peers than was Gary. By the end of grade nine, Gary was participating in some school social and extracur-ricular activities while Jay had quit school.

By the time Gary was born, much more information about ADD and behavior problems in general was available and adver-tised for parents. While much of the information and the attitudes of many toward Gary's problems were still more harmful than helpful, his parents were able to search out and find resources that were useful to the family in dealing with the problems. They were able to find books on hyperactivity, and their doctor suggested a trial of stimulant medication for Gary, then assessed the results. Luckily these were favorable. They were able to join a parent group where they could talk to and get support from other parents of ADD children. They were able to find a psychologist who offered family counselling in dealing with ADD and related problems and whom they felt helped them significantly in deal-ing with the school, neighbors and friends, and with family communication and discipline. All of these factors seem likely to have had a favorable effect on the outcome for Gary even though, according to his parents, he has shown no signs of outgrowing the ADD as yet.

Predictions from Older Research

Because the activity level of most hyperactive children decreases by adolescence, it was formerly believed that other problems did as well. It was commonly supposed that hyperac-tivity diminished during the teenage years and disappeared by adulthood. Yet, the adult picture for about one-half of formerly hyperactive children was bleak. Many as adults had difficulty holding a steady job and forming stable adult relationships. Some showed problems with alcohol or drugs or became depressed. Others developed other types of mental illness or became involved in crime (Ingersoll 1988, 20-21). Furthermore, research generally showed that none of the interventions tried during childhood — including medication, and counselling for the child and/or family — seemed to have any long-term effect on the outcome for the child. This, in spite of the fact that medication was clearly beneficial for many children while they were on it.

In looking at previous studies that have shown the ineffectiveness of treatment during childhood, certain problems have been pointed out and more recent research has attempted to take into account some of these factors (Moghadam 1988, 95-97). ADD children are a diverse group of individuals having different mixtures of symptoms to varying degrees. Because they vary so much, there are some who feel that outcomes may be different for various subgroups such as for those who are noticeably hyperactive, those who show strong aggression, or those who also have learning disabilities.

As well, in long-term studies such as these, many children from the original group are lost to follow-up for various reasons (Moghadam 1988, 95-96). Some specialists wonder if the prognosis for those lost to follow-up may be different than for those who remain in a study. It is suspected that those who are having more success with a treatment are more likely to stay in a project, while less successful cases may more readily drop out. As well, many studies have relied on parent reports as to whether prescribed treatments have been followed. It has been shown that parent reports aren't always reliable — even in reporting as to whether or not a child has taken medication as prescribed. Thus, conclusions based on such reporting are suspect. Another complicating factor when looking at evidence about the effectiveness of various treatments has been the short-term and sporadic nature of most treatment in the past. It is felt that treatment terms for most children in the past have been too short to have reasonably produced very much in the way of lasting results.

Realizing that there may be short-comings in such research, we can, nevertheless, look at a recent outcome study done in Canada at the Montreal Children's Hospital. A part of this study compared a group of twenty hyperactive children who had received at least three years treatment with stimulant medication to a group of untreated hyperactive children. In some areas such as school work and personality disorders, the treated group fared no better than their untreated counterparts. Yet, in other areas such as less car accidents, less delinquency, better social skills, better self-esteem and a more positive view of their childhood, those treated did better (Moghadam, p.99). This is encouraging information, particularly when combined with the new understanding that ADD children may benefit from an increased term of treatment, including into adulthood for as long as their symptoms persist.

New Ways of Looking at Adult ADD Problems

In the past, it was thought that children outgrew their hyperactivity though it was recognized that many of these children did not do well as adults. It is now recognized among experts that the ADD persists into adulthood for about one-half of ADD children (Ingersoll 1988, 20). ADD is now seen as comparable to diabetes. Treating the problem for awhile does not cure it. Rather, treatment is seen as replacement therapy which must be provided as long as the needed element is missing. Fortunately for some ADD children, chemical production or processes in the brain are thought to change as a child matures, and many outgrow their symptoms. However, for those who don't, the current way of looking at treatment may make a critical difference in their lives.

About one-half of ADD children will continue to have mild to severely disabling problems as adults. ADD that persists into adulthood has been labelled ADD-RT, this standing for attention deficit disorder — residual type (Wender 1987, 118). A necessary condition for the diagnosis of ADD-RT is that an individual must have had ADD as a child (appearance before age seven).

Psychiatrist and researcher, Paul H. Wender in *The Hyperactive Child, Adolescent, and Adult* describes research that he and colleagues, Dr. Frederick Reimherr and Dr. David Wood, have been involved in with ADD-RT individuals (Wender 1987). He cautions extreme care in diagnosing ADD-RT, in that other adult psychological disorders may have similar symptoms. It is particularly important that adults not try to diagnose themselves. Dr. Wender also points out that the findings he describes must be considered tentative until they are confirmed by other researchers. Although hyperactivity (excessive movement) is not necessary for the diagnosis of ADD, Dr. Wender and his colleagues have limited their research to ADD individuals who showed hyperactivity in childhood and continue to show it as adults because they wanted to study the most definite cases of ADD-RT.

In working with this limited group of ADD individuals, these doctors have found stimulant medication to be the most helpful treatment. Dr. Wender says it works for about two-thirds of their patients, and that results are sometimes dramatic (Wender 1987, 128). For many of these adults, counselling or therapy — which often takes the form of marital therapy — seems to be useful as well. These doctors also find it important to have a caring observer such as a wife or parent involved in treatment both for diagnosis and in evaluating the success of the treatment. This is because ADD adults, like ADD children, are often unaware of changes in their own behavior resulting from treatment.

Problems of ADD Adults

The difficulties that plagued these people as children take a slightly different form in adulthood and now the consequences of their behavior can be more serious, resulting in lost jobs and relationships, danger to themselves and others, and trouble with law enforcement agencies. ADD adults often continue to have problems paying attention to or concentrating on things they find uninteresting. This may cause them problems at work and in the family as well as socially when they have trouble keeping their minds on conversations. If hyperactivity persists, it may show as difficulty remaining seated for studying (if they continue their education) or a movie, and an impatience with tasks that require remaining sedentary. These adults may also feel restless much of the time, and engage in much toe-tapping and fidgetting.

Impulsivity can cause serious problems if ADD adults speed or gamble, without thinking about the consequences, or buy on impulse without sufficient money in the bank or realistic plans for payment. At work, they may impulsively engage in foolish schemes or speak their minds when they should be listening. Socially, they still tend to interrupt others and they may get into short-lived relationships. They are frequently bossy, strong-willed and stubborn (Wender 1987, 126). They may continue to experience mood swings over which they have little control and can get into serious problems with drug or alcohol abuse as well (Ingersoll 1988, 20).

Problems in disorganization may affect them both at home and at work as they skip from one task to another and have difficulty completing anything and finding needed items in their untidy workspaces. Their short tempers may now cause them to lose jobs, marriages and other personal relationships and may even cause child abuse or incidents of assault (Ingersoll 1988, 20). Because of these continuing problems, many ADD adults tend to be underachievers both at work and at home and their personal relationships tend to be stormy — this following their pattern as children (Wender 1987, 126).

Yet some ADD adults, in spite of continuing problems, do surprisingly well, particularly if they find a career that interests and challenges them and a mate that is caring and somewhat tolerant. For others, medication may be suggested to alleviate some of their troublesome symptoms and allow for happier lives for both them and their families. However, medication can have some of the same side effects it does in children, and cause other more serious problems.

Problems with Use of Medication for Adults

Dr. Wender explains that, as with children taking stimulant medication, adults may experience loss of appetite and/or have trouble getting to sleep at night. He also points out that with use of some medications there still may be several bad hours a day as the drug will not be effective before the morning dosage is taken or after it has worn off at night.

As well, these drugs can be abused. According to Dr. Wender if an adult escalates the dosage up to perhaps ten times to one hundred times the amount used to treat ADD, he can achieve a high from drug usage (Wender 1987, 133). Because some ADD adults have had previous problems with drug and/or alcohol abuse, doctors may understandably be reluctant to treat them with stimulant drugs which can be abused. Although they may not be as effective, other medications which are not so easily abused may be selected instead.

Considerations in Deciding on Medication for Adults

Dr. Wender, in weighing the possible benefits and harms of use of medication for adults, points out that the known risks for long-term treatment with stimulant medication are very low. In terms of allergies or negative reactions, he says these drugs appear safer than penicillin or aspirin (Wender 1987, 136-137).

He explains that the consequences of untreated ADD can be grave and severe both for the individual and society. The toll can be considerable in terms of jobs and marriages lost, abuse of alcohol or street drugs, depression and problems with the law.

He relates that ADD adults he has treated tend to request medication during periods when their lives become very difficult, then discontinue it until they hit serious trouble again. He warns that this may not be the wisest course because ADD adults do not readily perceive the effect of their behavior on others and may be causing extreme problems at work or in personal relationships before they realize things aren't going well. He recommends that the ADD adult be involved in therapy designed to help him become more aware of the effect on himself and others of his behavior before he attempts only periodic use of medication (Wender 1987, 137).

Family Influences on Adult Outcome

Experts are hopeful that a new emphasis on long-term, consistent treatment for the ADD child will improve his chances in adulthood — whether or not he outgrows his ADD. It would seem that a family that investigates avenues and is persistent in securing beneficial treatments for their child can increase his likelihood of a good adult adjustment. Besides such treatments and interventions, there are other complex and related family factors that seem to influence adult outcome for an ADD child.

Some of these elements can be termed "family support factors" as they involve experiences and situations within the family. Child-rearing practices and the parent-child relationship are important issues. As mentioned earlier, letting the child know often that you care about him and like him and finding time for fun can be of critical importance. Consistent, firm discipline is important, and harsh or excessive punishment, particularly physical punishment, can be extremely detrimental. A parent who seeks help in providing good management for a hyperactive child is not weak — but caring enough to get what is needed.

Family income and education level also seem to be important to the adult outcome for an ADD child as does the mental health of other family members. It may be that more affluent and educated parents have in the past sought help more readily and have had more money to spend on securing help for themselves and their child. However, it is possible to seek out help that is relatively inexpensive, and all parents owe it to themselves and their child to become as informed as possible about various options and to pursue those that are beneficial.

ADD Parents of ADD Children

Because ADD tends to run in families, there is a chance that one or both parents of an ADD child may have ADD themselves. It is more likely to be the father because of the predominance of males with this disorder. Whichever parent, an ADD adult may have difficulty providing the calmness and consistency which is best for the ADD child. As well, this disorder may be causing other problems in the adult's life and may have lowered his self-esteem, making it more difficult to deal with the stress of raising an ADD child.

Of course, it is also quite possible that an ADD parent, whether or not he has outgrown his ADD, will have more empathy with such a child and be more tolerant of his boisterousness and mistakes. He may remember techniques that others used with him that were helpful and use these to the benefit of his child. He may also be able to avoid for his child those things that were hurtful to him when he was young.

Conclusion

While the picture has not always been rosy for grown-up ADD individuals, there is much to be optimistic about in the newer research and information on ADD. About one-half of these children outgrow their ADD by the time they reach adulthood and usually do well as adults — it is now believed they may fare even better if their treatment has been adequate during childhood. ADD children usually have many positive qualities as well as high energy and drive which they may be able to use to their advantage. Some ADD adults do considerably better in adulthood than they did during school and childhood because of the diversity of options available to adults, and because they have learned ways to compensate for their difficulties.

Research has clearly shown that the functioning of many ADD children improves while they are on medication. Benefits to ADD children have been shown from behavioral interventions as well. Some experts have new hope that long-term treatment during childhood may improve the characteristics ADD children take into adulthood. For those adults with significant disabilities, it is now proposed that symptoms can often be controlled for as long as the disorder persists.

Awareness of parents, teachers and the public is rising as information becomes available on the nature of ADD. Doctors and other professionals appear to increasingly favor extended treatment. The child is now likely to experience less blame and failure and to have greater recognition of the problems he has with self-esteem.

Even though the answers and the options have improved, there will still be considerable fortitude required in dealing with the day to day problems of an ADD child. I believe it important that families and others working with ADD children keep an open, enquiring, optimistic attitude toward new information on ADD which may help them.

As a final word to parents, I would like to reiterate that a strong, supportive family can be of crucial importance in the life of an ADD child. This means parents can waste no energy on the debilitating effects of blaming others or themselves or on soul-searching as to what they might have done differently. It is likely that parents have been angry and blaming toward an ADD child, and have failed in some ways (as have most parents). Self-reproach may be natural and difficult to shake, but it is a monkey that those who have the onerous task of raising an ADD child do not need on their backs. Accept that you are human and have done your best for your child in the past, and will continue to do so in the future. You owe it to your child to forgive yourself and others for mistakes you or they may have made. Then your energy will be freed to support your child and to locate and implement interventions which can help him grow into a happy, productive adult.

Appendix:
Finding Help for ADD

Questions for Parents and Professionals

Separate chapters in this book have dealt with the diagnosis of ADD and various treatment options and interventions parents might seek through medical, mental health and educational professionals. It has been pointed out that professionals may have difficulty diagnosing ADD because many of the behavioral symptoms can appear to have been caused by faulty discipline, poor family dynamics or traumatic experiences. Obviously, individual professionals will have varying knowledge about ADD and various degrees of difficulty in differentiating ADD from other problems. As well, it has been mentioned that ADD is underdiagnosed at present for a variety of reasons, including a belief by some professionals that ADD children always move a lot, and disagreement as to the severity of symptoms a child must display.

Understandably, professionals are hesitant to put a label on a child, and we as parents do not want to advertise our child as having disabilities. Our main concern is getting help for our child and family. Unfortunately, in order to get some types of treatments (notably medication), and for some professionals to understand the nature of problems our child and family are experiencing, a label may be necessary. If this is so, we must not lose sight of the fact that the child is much more normal than disabled and is a unique individual who, just like other individuals, has many strengths as well as weaknesses, even though some of his problems fall into a particular category.

Once ADD has been diagnosed, there is still considerable controversy among professionals as to the treatments and interventions helpful to the child and family. Sensationalistic reports in the press about ADD and, in particular, about the use of stimulant medication as a means of helping the child normalize his behavior may have influenced the views of some professionals, and there are some professionals who don't use particular treatments as a matter of principle (although they may believe them to be effective).

Thus, parents of a child who is having difficulties of the kind described in this book and who are seeking help for these problems will want to investigate the beliefs and approaches of professionals they contact. They will want to assess the professional's familiarity and experience in treating a wide range of behavior problems in children, including ADD. It may be that your child's difficulties are not due to ADD, and will need a different approach than that described in this book. Yet, if you suspect your child may have ADD, you will want to find professionals you feel have the expertise and experience to accurately diagnose ADD and provide the most useful treatments. Experts in ADD have suggested that all professionals are not equally competent in diagnosing and treating this disorder, and have suggested that parents might need to seek a referral to a specialist in the area of childhood behavior disorders.

If, in fact, your child is found to have ADD, the three general areas where various professionals can provide help in dealing with some of the problems related to ADD are illustrated in Figure 2. A team consisting of at least one medical person, one mental health professional, and one person with expertise in educational interventions can often be most helpful to the child and family in dealing with ADD and associated problems. (This team should also be capable of dealing with specific learning disabilities should these be present.) However, few regions have such a team readily accessible to families, so in most cases parents will have to seek their own team of medical, psychological and educational experts. There are cases, too, where not all these types of input will be needed.

Before seeking diagnosis and treatment for ADD, it is advisable for parents to become familiar with literature on ADD regarding causes, diagnosis and treatment, so they will better understand information given by professionals. Keeping in mind that they, themselves, are the experts on the difficuties and temperament of their child, parents can discuss problems and tactfully ask questions of those they contact. One must, however, use discretion and keep in mind the point of view and possible reservations of some professionals. Doctors are often wary of

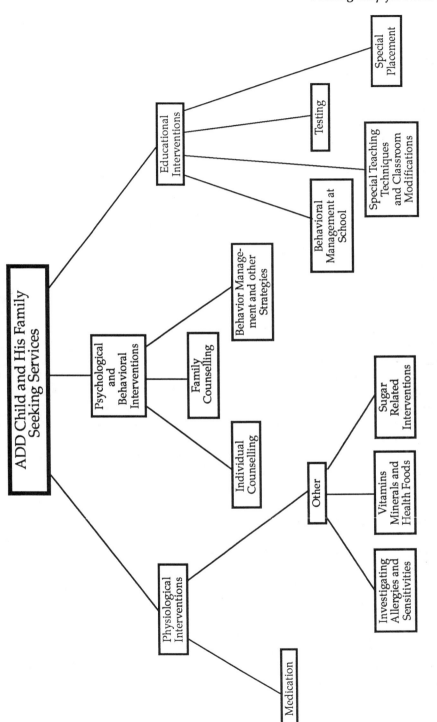

Figure 2

patients who come in, magazine or book in hand, sure that they have the latest malady described and that they are in need of the undertested or overdramatized treatment that has been described. Professionals may resent patients whom they feel have diagnosed their own problems and are leading the doctor to a particular conclusion. Suspicion may be aroused if they feel parents are taking a child from practioner to practitioner looking for the "right" diagnosis. Also some doctors and other professionals resent being questioned directly about their knowledge, views or treatments, feeling, perhaps, that one is suggesting a lack of competence.

Keeping this in mind, I believe it is a parent's responsibility and right to try to find the most helpful (in the broadest sense) treatments and interventions for their child's and family's problems. At the same time, they must keep in mind the controversy over ADD and that there are at present no totally satisfactory answers to ADD. Often the most helpful practitioners will be those who offer options to be tried without guarantee of success.

Following is a list of questions parents who suspect their child may have ADD can use as a guide in seeking out professionals most capable of diagnosing and treating ADD. Remember, it is important to enter into discussion with such professionals — sharing concerns and seeking opinions and answers rather than interrogating professionals and looking for predetermined answers. Later you can reflect on the adequacy of information and views you have been given and decide if you need to seek alternate advice. Professionals might use these questions in a self-evaluation of the type and extent of expertise and services they are able to provide ADD children and their families.

Diagnosis and Treatment of ADD:
Questions for Professionals

1. Has this professional diagnosed and treated ADD children before? Has he worked with a lot of such children and their families?

2. What tests and procedures does she use in diagnosis? Is she willing to explain methods she uses to diagnose and tell what she might be looking for?

3. What might these tests and procedures show that is specific to ADD? How does he tell ADD from other behavior or learning problems?

4. How fully will she share test results with parents?

5. What is this practitioner's view as to the cause of ADD?

6. What are the treatments and interventions (medical, psychological, and/or educational) he might recommend for ADD? If a medical doctor, does he sometimes prescribe medication? If another professional, does he agree with the use of medication for ADD?

7. Are there side-effects of any treatments?

8. How does she monitor treatment and intervention success and problems?

9. Is he willing to fully communicate his findings and views about this child's case with the parents?

10. Is she willing to communicate and work with other professionals working with the family?

11. Is he willing to provide a copy to parents of any written communication with other professsionals about this child?

References

American Psychiatric Association. *Diagnostic and Statistical Manual of Mental Disorders*, Third Edition, Revised. Washington, DC: American Psychiatric Association, 1987.

Barkley, R.A. "Attention Deficit Disorders." In *Handbook of Clinical Behavior Therapy with Children*. Edited by P.H. Bornstein and A.E. Kazdin. Homewood, Illinois: Dorsey Press, 1985, pp. 158-217.

Betts, G.T. and M. Neihart. "Profiles of the Gifted and Talented." *Gifted Child Quarterly*, 32, 2 (Spring, 1988): 248-253.

Camp, Bonnie W. and Mary Ann S. Bash. *Think Aloud: Increasing Social and Cognitive Skills — A Problem-Solving Program for Children*. Champaign, Illinois: Research Press, 1985.

Colangelo, N. "Myths and Stereotypes of Gifted Students: Awareness for the Classroom Teacher." In *Multicultural Nonsexist Education: A Human Relations Approach*. Edited by N. Colangelo, C.H. Foxley, and R. Dustin. Dubuque, Iowa: Kendall/Hunt Publishers, 1979.

Colangelo, N. and Cynthia B. Dowdall. "Underachieving Gifted Students: Review and Implications." *Gifted Child Quarterly*, 26, 4 (Fall, 1982).

DeMille, Richard. *Put Your Mother on the Ceiling: Children's Imagination Games*. Markham, Ont: Penguin Books Canada Ltd., 1976.

Dreikurs, Rudolph. *Psychology in the Classroom*. New York: Harper and Row, 1957.

Ellis, A. and R.A Harper. *A New Guide to Rational Living*. Hollywood, California: Wiltshire Book Company, 1975.

Feingold, B.F. *Why Your Child Is Hyperactive*. New York: Random House, 1975.

Friedrick, B.A. "ADD: A Common Cause of Problems at School." *Early Childhood Education*, 22, 1 (Winter, 1988-89): 17-18.

Gallucci, Nicholas. "Emotional Adjustment of Gifted Children." *Gifted Child Quarterly*, 32, 2 (Spring, 1988): 267-272.

Gattozzi, R. *What's Wrong with My Child?* New York: McGraw-Hill Book Company, 1986.

Gold, S.J. *When Children Invite Child Abuse: A Search for Answers When Love is not Enough*. Eugene, Oregon: Fern Ridge Press, 1986.

Green, K. Fine, M.J. and N. Tollefson. "Family Systems Characteristics and Underachieving Gifted Adolescent Males." *Gifted Child Quarterly*, 32, 2 (Spring, 1988): 267-272.

Hollands, E.A. *How A Mother Copes with Hyperactivity*. Altona, Manitoba: D.W. Frieson and Sons Ltd., 1983.

Homme, Lloyd et al. *How to Use Contingency Contracting in the Classroom*. Champaign, Illinois, Research Press, 1970.

Ingersoll, B. *Your Hyperactive Child: A Parent's Guide to Coping with Attention Deficit Disorder*. New York: Doubleday, 1988.

Kinsbourne, M. and J.M. Swanson, "Hyperactivity." In *Anything Can Be: The Identification and Remediation of Learning Disabilities in the Classroom*. Edited by GEMS Educational Materials and Seminars. Ottawa, Ontario: Canadian Association for Children with Learning Disabilities, 1983, pp. 93-105.

Krupski, A. "Attentional Problems in Youngsters with Learning Handicaps." In *Psychological and Educational Perspectives on Learning Disabilities*. Edited by J.K. Torgesen and B.Y.L. Wong. San Diego, California: Academic Press Inc., 1986, pp. 161-192.

Leverton, S.M. "Toward Positive Social Behavior in ADD-H Children." *Early Childhood Education*, 22, 1 (Winter, 1988): 19-21.

Lieberman, L.M. *Special Educator's Guide to Regular Education*. Weston, Mass.: Nobb Hill Press Inc., 1986.

Moghadam, H. *Attention Deficit Disorder: Hyperactivity Revisited*. Calgary, Alberta: Detselig Enterprises Ltd., 1988.

Pelham, W.E. Jr. "The Effects of Psychostimulant Drugs on Learning and Academic Achievement in Children with Attention Deficit Disorders and Learning Disabilities." In *Psychological and Educational Perspectives on Learning Disabilities*. Edited by J.K. Torgesen and B.Y.L. Wong. San Diego, California: Academic Press Inc., 1986, pp. 259-295.

Renzulli, Joseph S. *The Enrichment Triad Model: A Guide for Developing Defensible Programs for the Gifted and Talented*. Mansfield Center, Connecticut: Creative Learning Press, Inc., 1977.

Restak, Richard M. *The Mind: The Official Companion Volume to the Landmark PBS Television Series*. New York: Bantam Books, 1988.

Sawrey, James M. and Charles W. Telford. *Educational Psychology*. Boston, Mass.: Allyn and Bacon, Inc., 1958.

Silver, L.B. *The Misunderstood Child: A Guide for Parents of Learning Disabled Children*. New York: McGraw-Hill Book Company, 1988.

Smith, L.H. *Improving Your Child's Behavior Chemistry.* Englewood Cliffs, N.J.: Prentice-Hall Inc., 1976.

Stewart, M.A. and Olds, S.W. *Raising a Hyperactive Child.* New York: Harper and Row, 1973.

Turecki, Stanley and Leslie Tonner. *The Difficult Child.* New York: Bantam Books, 1989.

Truch, Stephen. *Teacher Burnout and What to do About it.* Novato, California: Academic Therapy Publications, 1980.

Vitale, Barbara Meister. *Unicorns Are Real: A Right-Brained Approach to Learning.* Rolling Hills Estates, California: Jalmar Press, 1982.

Wender, P.H. *The Hyperactive Child, Adolescent, and Adult: Attention Deficit Disorder Through the Lifespan.* New York: Oxford University Press, 1987.

Whitmore, Joanne R. "Gifted Children with Handicapping Conditions: A New Frontier." *Exceptional Children,* 48, 2 (October, 1988): 106-112.

Williams, Linda VerLee. *Teaching for the Two-Sided Mind: A Guide to Right Brain/Left Brain Education.* New York: Simon & Schuster, Inc., 1983.

Notes

Notes

Notes

Printed in Canada